W9-BYA-211

LIVING IN THE LIGHT
MONEY, SEX & POWER

JOHN PIPER

LIVING IN THE LIGHT
MONEY
SEX &
POWER

*Making the most of
three dangerous opportunities*

Living in the Light: Money, Sex & Power
By John Piper © Desiring God Foundation, 2016

Published by
The Good Book Company
Tel (North America): (1) 866 244 2165
Tel (UK): 0333 123 0880
International: +44 (0) 208 942 0880
Email (North America): info@thegoodbook.com
Email (UK): info@thegoodbook.co.uk

Websites
North America: www.thegoodbook.com
UK & Europe: www.thegoodbook.co.uk
Australia: www.thegoodbook.com.au
New Zealand: www.thegoodbook.co.nz

Unless otherwise indicated, Scripture quotations are from The Holy Bible, English Standard Version (ESV), copyright © 2001 by Crossway, a publishing ministry of Good News Publishers. Used by permission. All rights reserved.

All rights reserved. Except as may be permitted by the Copyright Act, no part of this publication may be reproduced in any form or by any means without prior permission from the publisher.

ISBN: 9781784980511

Printed by Nørhaven, Denmark

Design by André Parker

Cover design by Ben Woodcraft

To Richard Coekin
and Co-Mission
with admiration and thankfulness

CONTENTS

INTRODUCTION

God did not conceive and create money, sex, and power simply to be a temptation. He had good purposes in mind.

Money, sex, and power exist for the great aims of God in human history. They are not detours on the path to God-exalting joy. Along with all the rest of God's good world, they are the path. With them, we can show the supreme worth of God.

To show how that happens is one of the aims of this book. Therefore, the approach I take is to pursue the potentials of money, sex, and power as well as the pitfalls. What are the dangers that need to be defeated? What are their potentials, which need to be deployed?

The main thesis of the book has two parts. First, that money, sex, and power, which began as God's good gifts to humanity, have become dangerous because all human beings have exchanged the glory of God for images (Romans 1 v 23). Second, that money, sex, and power will be restored to their God-glorifying place by the redemption that God brought into the world through Jesus Christ—the great liberation of creation from all sin and sickness and sorrow.

Without that redemption, all of us prefer other things to God. That's our nature. When we stop to think about it, we realize that this is a great insult to God. In fact, preferring anything to God is a moral outrage in the universe—and therefore it is an eternal threat to our souls. Not only will this preference for anything over God destroy us, it also leads to a pervasive distortion of all that is good in the world, including money, sex, and power.

All of creation was meant to communicate the supreme beauty and worth of God (Psalm 19 v 1; Romans 1 v 20-23). God created the world for his glory (Isaiah 43 v 7). He created the world so that he would be magnified by the way his creatures find their greatest satisfaction in him. Money, sex, and power exist ultimately to show that God is more to be desired than money, sex, and power. That is, paradoxically, how they become most satisfying in themselves.

All of this was ruined by the fall—by the first great folly of exchanging God for other things. When

God is restored as the supreme value of the human heart, money, sex, and power begin to find their God-glorifying place in life. Everything hangs on what we value as supreme. What is our highest treasure? What is our greatest satisfaction? When God takes that place in our minds and hearts—in our thoughts and our emotions—then money, sex, and power begin to find their true and beautiful order.

This new ordering of life, with God's glory at the center, turns out to be the most satisfying to our souls (though embattled in many ways), most beneficial for the world (though it may not always see this), and most honoring to God. We are satisfied. The world is served. And God is glorified. That is what money, sex, and power are made for. And that is what this book is about.

DEFINITIONS AND FOUNDATIONS

When I say "money, sex, and power," what, exactly, do I mean?

What I have found over the years is that the effort to define things, at the beginning, almost always reveals that what we thought we were dealing with is merely the tip of an iceberg. We thought we were dealing with money—paper currency and coins. But in fact, underneath we're dealing with the pleasures and advantages money can buy, or the status money can signify. And then we realize, no, that's not the bottom, because underneath that is covetousness, greed, fear, and cravings for safety, prestige or control. Then again, no, that's not the bottom either, because the Bible teaches us that there is another reality—a condition of the heart—deeper than all those sins.

We realize—just by trying to define what we are talking about—that this thing called money or sex or power is like the fraction of an iceberg we can see above the water. It's not the problem. What we can see isn't going to sink our boat. It's those massive, jagged, saw-tooth ridges of sin below the waterline that will put a gash in the hull and send us to the bottom of the ocean.

Then, as I sit and ponder the definitions of money, sex, and power with the help of some thoughtful friends (this happened to me as I was preparing these chapters of the book), I realize that I have just used an image that sets up the whole thing in a totally negative way, and that I missed an even more foundational reality.

ICEBERGS OR FLOATING ISLANDS?

What about money that we use to support a missionary, or buy a gift for a friend? What about the underlying generosity that is in that? And what about the heart that produces it? The bad tree produces bad fruit—but what about the good tree that produces good fruit (Matthew 7 v 16-19)? So it turns out that money, sex, and power are not always an iceberg about to sink our boat. They may be floating islands of food when the stores of our ship have run out, or fuel when we are stalled in the water, or the rarest fruit to sweeten our dreary sailing diet.

In other words, another foundational reality we have to deal with is that money, sex, and power are, from the beginning, gifts of God—good gifts of God. And if they sink us, it isn't because God gave us bad gifts; it's because something happened inside us to turn gifts of grace into instruments of sin, into altars and incense in the temple of pride.

So the first thing we need to do is talk about definitions which lead us to see certain foundational realities that are far deeper—and far bigger—than the dangerous icebergs or the floating treasure-islands of money, sex, and power. That's what this first chapter is about—definitions and foundations.

Then from the second to the fourth chapters, we will focus on the peculiar dangers of money, sex, and power (the icebergs). In the fifth and sixth chapters, we will focus on how the gospel delivers us from the icebergs, and frees us to enjoy the peculiar potential (the treasure-islands) of money, sex, and power as we deploy them in the cause of Christ-exalting love and worship. So that's the plan: Definitions and foundations. Dangers and how to defeat them. Potentials and how to deploy them. Define. Defeat. Deploy.

MONEY: DEFINITION AND FOUNDATION

We start with money. Money, in its simplest form, is some kind of currency. It might be paper, or metal; in other cultures, perhaps, stones, or in our culture, electronic records. This currency functions as a culturally defined representation of quantities of value, so that the currency can be used to pursue something you want, by spending it, giving it, or keeping it.

The currency itself is a good gift from God that you can turn for evil or for good. You can spend it to get something you value, like food, a gift, a lottery ticket, or a prostitute. You can give it away to advance some cause that you value, like a young person going on a mission trip, or to maintain a secret with someone who is blackmailing you, or by getting a job through bribery. Or you can keep it to solidify some value that you have, like the security of a thick financial cushion, or saving wisely for a future purchase to avoid debt.

In other words, money—the symbolic representation of quantities of value—becomes a moral issue because of the rightness or wrongness of what you pursue with this gift God has given you. You can pursue good, and you can pursue evil. You can use it to show that you value money more than Christ. Or you can use it to show that you value Christ more than money.

This means that the currency itself is not the issue we must wrestle with. There is something much more foundational, something far deeper than wealth or poverty—far deeper than greed or generosity. In sum, then, money is one cultural symbol that we use to show what we value. It is a means by which we show where our treasure is; who our treasure is. The use of money is an act of worship—either of Christ, or of something else.

SEX: DEFINITION AND FOUNDATION

By "sex" I mean experiencing erotic stimulation, seeking to get the experience, or seeking to give the experience. And when I say that, I mean that sex is a good gift from God in all those ways. Experiencing sexual stimulation, seeking to have it, or seeking to give it— all three are God's good gifts, which we may enjoy as he appointed, or exploit to our eventual harm.

Three clarifications are in order. First, I know that the word "sexual" can be used much more broadly than this. A husband and a wife may have deep and wonderful conversations, for example, or shared activities, that are sexual in the broad sense that she is female and he is male, and those conversations and activities may have no erotic element—but are wonderfully laden with subtle enjoyments that are not identical, but complementary, to our sexuality. That's true, and that is wonderful. But I'm not talking about that. Limitations keep this book short.

A second clarification is that I have in mind a broad range of sexual activity from the most casual and even accidental stimulation to the most intense and intentional stimulation. A man may have mildly erotic thoughts about a woman worship leader when she has no intention to cause that at all. Or a woman may have sexual feelings about a pastor, wishing her husband were more spiritually passionate, and that pastor may have no intention or desire for such a thing. I am including all those experiences in what I mean by "sex."

One more clarification. This means that sex, as I mean it, may be happening when there is no erotic effect whatsoever, because the one trying to stimulate the other (for example, by how he or she acts or dresses) may not succeed at all. So by my definition, "sex" would be happening, but no one is getting any sexual pleasure.

The experience of erotic stimulation itself, and the effort to get it or give it, may be a good use of God's good gift, or a merely selfish exploitation. What makes sex virtuous or a vice is not the pleasure, or the pursuit (to give it or get it), but something deeper. There are foundational issues of submission to the word of God and the condition of the heart. That's what we will need to look at, if we are going to say anything helpful about the pitfalls and potential of this divine gift of sex.

POWER: DEFINITION AND FOUNDATION

Power is the capacity to get what you want. The capacity may lie in the fact that you have great physical strength; or that you have a position of authority, like a parent, teacher, policeman, or Member of Congress. Or it may lie in the fact that you have more money than anyone in the group, or that you are very beauti ful or handsome.

All of those capacities are good gifts of God. We don't have any of them solely by our own design or effort. God is the decisive Giver of them all. And all those capacities to get what you want can be used to do evil or to do good. How you use your power shows where your heart is, what you love, what you treasure most—what you worship.

WHAT MONEY, SEX, AND POWER HAVE IN COMMON

Perhaps it's becoming clear why I didn't structure this book in three separate sections: one on money, the next on sex, and the third on power. The reason is that at root—at the foundations—they are fundamentally the same. They are ways of displaying God's supreme worth in your life, or they are ways of displaying what you think is the supreme worth of something else. The way you think and feel and act about money, sex, and power puts your heart's treasure on display—either God, or something he made.

- Power is a capacity to pursue what you value.
- Money is a cultural symbol that can be exchanged in pursuit of what you value.
- Sex is one of the pleasures that people value, and the pursuit of it.

Therefore power, money and sex are all God-given means of showing what you value. They are (like all other created reality in the universe) given by God as means of worship—that is, as means of magnifying what is of supreme worth to you. All your power, all your money and all your sexuality are God's gifts for putting on display the supreme worth of God's glory.

TURNING TO THE FOUNDATIONS

You can see that we have moved somewhat beyond definitions, down to the foundations that reveal what money, sex, and power are really about in a God-centered universe like ours. What we need to do now is go to the Bible and see how God makes clear what these foundational issues are.

What, at root, are we created to be? What are we created to do with the good gifts of money, sex, and power? And what's wrong with us at root, that instead of putting the worth of God on display with our money, sex, and power, we, by nature, actually make him disappear, as if the Creator and Sustainer of everything were inconsequential? That is the greatest outrage in the world. Christ came to turn that around—in your life, and in this world.

WHAT IS THE CONDITION OF THE HUMAN HEART?

In Romans 1 v 18-23, we find a description of our deepest human problem, and the greatest glory from which we have fallen—the glory we can return to in Christ. The apostle Paul drills down beneath sinful actions to the heart that sins. He drills down through destructive behaviors to depraved hearts—my heart and yours:

> [18] The wrath of God is revealed from heaven against all ungodliness and unrighteousness of men, who by their unrighteousness suppress the truth. [19] For what can be known about God is plain to them, because God has shown it to them. [20] For his invisible

attributes, namely, his eternal power and divine nature, have been clearly perceived, ever since the creation of the world, in the things that have been made. So they are without excuse. [21] For although they knew God, they did not honor him as God or give thanks to him, but they became futile in their thinking, and their foolish hearts were darkened. [22] Claiming to be wise, they became fools, [23] and exchanged the glory of the immortal God for images resembling mortal man and birds and animals and creeping things.

Let's start with verse 18. "The wrath of God is revealed from heaven against all ungodliness and unrighteousness of men, who by their unrighteousness suppress the truth." Paul describes mankind in general as "ungodly" and "unrighteous." That is our condition. All of us.

When Paul finishes his analysis of the human condition, he sums up in Romans 3 v 9: "What then? Are we Jews any better off? No, not at all. For we have already charged that all, both Jews and Greeks, are under sin." We are all in this condition of "ungodly" and "unrighteous."

And the first thing Paul says about this condition is that it causes people to suppress the truth: "By their unrighteousness [they] suppress the truth" (1 v 18).

Another way to describe what happens is that we intentionally blind ourselves to the light of truth. The theme of this book, remember, is *Living in the Light: Money, Sex & Power*. Living in the light. Right here in Romans 1, we are seeing why this is so crucial.

Sin repels the light of truth and runs to the darkness of falsehood. Jesus said that we are sinners not because we are victims of the darkness but because we are lovers of the darkness: "Light has come into the world, and people loved the darkness rather than the light" (John 3 v 19).

The first mark of our sinful nature is that it inclines us, and empowers us, to suppress the truth—to hate the light.

WHAT DO WE SUPPRESS?

What specific truth, what "light," does our sinful nature hate? The next verse tells us. "For what can be known about God is plain to them, because God has shown it to them" (Romans 1 v 19). We suppress "what can be known about God." Knowledge of God is repulsive to our sinful nature. Our deepest problem is not ignorance. Verse 19 says, "What can be known about God is plain." Our deepest problem is that we revolt against the knowledge of God. It is offensive to us. It undermines our independence and autonomy.

We see it again in verse 20—our deepest problem is not ignorance of God: "His invisible attributes, namely, his eternal power and divine nature, have been clearly perceived, ever since the creation of the world, in the things that have been made." And again, in verse 21: "Although they knew God…" Our problem is not ignorance. Our problem is that in our unrighteousness we suppress the truth. We hate the light, and we love the darkness, and so we do not want to walk in the light of truth.

So at the end of verse 20, Paul says, "They are without excuse." Why? Verse 21 gives the answer that goes to the root of the problem: "For although they knew God, they did not honor him as God or give thanks to him, but they became futile in their thinking, and their foolish hearts were darkened." We did not glorify him as God, nor did we thank him. We chose the darkness of man-exaltation over God-exaltation. This is what we do by nature.

Our sinful hearts do not love to glorify God—to treasure God as glorious, delight in God as supremely beautiful, and display God as our greatest treasure. Our sinful hearts do not want to treasure God as glorious and thank him for everything. That's what the word "ungodly" means in verse 18 ("the wrath of God is revealed from heaven against all ungodliness … of men"). In our "ungodliness," we do what ungodliness does—it suppresses the truth that God is to be treasured as supremely glorious and generous. Our sinful nature hates the light of God's supremacy and runs to the darkness, where we feel supreme.

When the truth is suppressed, and the light is rejected, and the glory of God is disregarded, something else always takes their place. The human heart hates a vacuum. We never merely leave God because we value him little; we always exchange God for what we value more. We see this in verses 22-23: "Claiming to be wise, they became fools, and exchanged the glory of the immortal God for images." They became fools. This is the ultimate foolishness. This is the most foundational meaning of sin: exchanging the glory of the immortal God for substitutes—anything we value more than God. If you have ears to hear, this should sound like the ultimate stupidity and the ultimate outrage—that we consider God, reject him as our supreme treasure, and trade him away. We look at the Creator and then exchange him for something he created.

Underneath all the misuses of money, sex, and power is this sinful heart-condition—this depravity. My definition of sin, based on this passage in Romans 1, is this: sin is any feeling or thought or action that comes from a heart that does not treasure God over all other things. The bottom of sin, the root of all sins, is such a heart—a heart that prefers anything above God; a heart that does not treasure God over everything else, and everyone else.

DEEP AND PERVASIVE

Sin is the deepest, strongest and most pervasive problem of the human race. In fact, once Paul has made clear what the essence or root of sin is in Romans 1 – 3, he goes on to make clear in the following chapters the magnitude of its power in us. He speaks of sin reigning like a king in death (5 v 21); holding dominion like a lord (6 v 14); enslaving like a slavemaster (6 v 6, 16-17, 20) to whom we have been sold (7 v 14); as a force that produces other sins (7 v 8); as a power that seizes the law and kills (7 v 11); as a hostile occupying tenant that dwells in us (7 v 17, 20); and as a law that takes us captive (7 v 23).

All that deep, strong, pervasive reality of sin in us defines us until we are born again. That miracle must happen, or this deep antagonism toward God will go on controlling and directing us forever. Jesus put it this way: "That which is born of the flesh is flesh, and that which is born of the Spirit is spirit. Do not

marvel that I said to you, 'You must be born again'"
(John 3 v 6-7). By virtue of our first birth, we are
merely flesh—that is, we are devoid of God's Spirit
and life. But when we are "born of the Spirit," God's
Spirit gives us spiritual life and moves into us, and we
have life in him forever.

That life comes with the light of truth. "Jesus spoke
to them, saying, 'I am the light of the world. Whoever
follows me will not walk in darkness, but will have the
light of life'" (John 8 v 12). Eternal life and true light
are always together. We "live in the light" when the
Spirit gives us life.

To underline the serious bondage we are in before
this new birth, Paul goes on to say in Romans, "Nothing good dwells in me, that is, in my flesh" (7 v 18).
What we are apart from new birth—new creation by
the Spirit of God because of Christ—is the embodi-
ment of resistance to God. "The mind that is set on
the flesh is hostile to God, for it does not submit to
God's law; indeed, it cannot" (8 v 7). Why can't it?
Because it doesn't want to. We disapprove of God as
supreme (1 v 28). We exchange him, because we prefer
other things more.

So we must lay to rest forever the notion that our
sin is mainly what we do. It's not: it is mainly who we

are—until we are a new creature in Christ. And even then, it is an ever-present, indwelling enemy to be put to death every day by the Spirit (7 v 17, 20, 23; 8 v 13).

Before Christ, sin is not an alien power in us. Sin is our preference for anything over God. Sin is our disapproval of God. Sin is our exchange of his glory for substitutes. Sin is our suppression of the truth of God. Sin is our heart's hostility to God. It is who we are to the bottom of our hearts. Until Christ.

Against this bleak description of the root of our problem in the handling of money, sex, and power, what also becomes clear is that this distortion of our souls is not what we were made to be. We were meant to know God and to glorify and thank him (1 v 19-21). We were meant to see him, and, by seeing him, reflect his own beauty. We were to do that not by exchanging him for something, but by preferring him over everything. We were to glorify God by treasuring him over all treasures, enjoying him over all pleasures, desiring him over all desires, prizing him over all prizes, wanting him over all wants.

TWO POSSIBLE CONDITIONS
These are the two great heart-conditions in human life: the heart that values God over all, or values

something else more. One heart is happy in the light of God's supreme worth. The other heart is happy in the darkness, fondling images of the real thing, thinking we have found a great treasure. The mark of the true Christian is not that sin never gets the upper hand—not that our desires are flawlessly Godward. The mark of the Christian is that at the root of our lives is this new treasuring of God over all things, as we have met him in Jesus Christ. He has assumed a place in our hearts that pulls us back again and again to renew our devotion to him as supreme. Christians have discovered that the indwelling Spirit magnifies the worth of Jesus above all things, and moves us to repentance when we fail to feel that worth as we ought. "If we confess our sins, he is faithful and just to forgive us our sins and to cleanse us from all un-righteousness" (1 John 1 v 9).

Money, sex, and power are three good gifts of God. In the next three chapters, we will see that we can use them to reveal a heart of darkness, or reveal a heart of light. And in doing so, we will reveal the truth of God's supreme beauty and worth, or we will portray him as inadequate for our soul's desire. We can have a heart that treasures this world above God, or a heart that treasures God above this world. And thus we can glorify God as all-satisfying, or defame him as inferior to the things he has made. We can live in the light, or in the darkness.

2

THE PLEASURE-DESTROYING DANGERS OF SEX

When Satan wanted to destroy Adam and Eve's supreme pleasure in the sinless enjoyment of God's friendship, he did not present them with a duty, but with a delight.

They saw that the tree from which God had forbidden them to eat was "good for food, and that it was a delight to the eyes, and that the tree was to be desired to make one wise"—and so they took and ate (Genesis 3 v 6). The pathway to the destruction of their pleasure was "good" and a "delight" and a "desire." And Satan's trick was to make the fruit look more desirable than God. It worked.

Sexual pleasure is forbidden as an alternative to pleasure in God. That's the way to see its relation to the tree in the Garden of Eden. God ought to be treasured above sexual pleasure, and tasted in sexual pleasure. The very delights and passions and ecstasies of God-designed sexual intercourse in marriage are the kinds of pleasure God himself conceived and created. They come from him. They are something of him. He is that kind of pleasure-knowing, pleasure-imagining, pleasure-creating God. And therefore when we taste those pleasures, we are tasting something of God. He made sexual pleasure, and so he is greater. And he made it to communicate something of himself. He never meant it to be an alternative to pleasure in him. He meant for himself to be seen and savored in it. If God ceases to be treasured above, and tasted in, sexual pleasure, it becomes poisonous—just like the fruit of the tree in the garden.

LOSING THE LIGHT

We are picking up where we left off in the previous chapter in dealing with Romans 1. With stunning relevance to our own day, Paul makes the connection for us between exchanging the light of God for darkness on the one hand, and the distortion and destructiveness of sexual sin on the other. We begin the "Dangers" section with a chapter on the dangers of sex because Paul himself makes it a doorway into the dangers of all misuses of God's gifts. Sex becomes the test case that reveals what money, sex, and power have in common in terms of their dangers. Paul intends for us to see that what we discover about abandoning light and distorting sex will apply to money and power as well.

We start with Romans 1 v 21-23:

> [21] Although they knew God, they did not honor him as God or give thanks to him, but they became futile in their thinking, and their foolish hearts were darkened. [22] Claiming to be wise, they became fools, [23] and exchanged the glory of the immortal God for images resembling mortal man and birds and animals and creeping things.

The word "light" is not used in these verses. But the word "darkness" is, at the end of verse 21: "Their foolish hearts were darkened." And instead of contrasting that darkness with light, Paul contrasts it with glory—the light and the brightness of God's beauty and perfections. "They did not honor him as God" (or "glorify," NIV, v 21) but instead they "exchanged the glory of God for images" (v 23). So he is saying that, in our sinful, unregenerate condition, we know God in one sense ("although they knew God," v 21); nevertheless, we take the glory of God, so to speak, and trade it. We exchange it. And in doing so, we push away the light of the universe—the divine brightness, and beauty, and meaning of created reality—and consign ourselves to darkness. In Eden, Adam and Eve thought they were choosing wisdom and life, but they were choosing darkness and death. "Claiming to be wise, they became fools" (v 22). And we have been doing that ever since.

So living in darkness means seeing God as minimally desirable, and seeing his creation as maximally desirable. That's implied in the word "exchanged." They exchanged the glory of God. When you exchange something, you express your preference. You express your greater desire. And if you prefer God's creation over God, then you find God less desirable than what you prefer. And that is what it means to be in the darkness. The darkness is where you can't see things for what they really are. If you see anything as more beautiful, more attractive, more desirable than God, you are in the dark. You are not seeing reality for what it is.

Living in the light is seeing God as supremely glorious, supremely beautiful, supremely desirable, and supremely satisfying. If we were living in the light, we would never exchange his glory because we would see things clearly. We would cherish his glory and keep it at any cost.

He would be more precious to us than anything. That's what it means to live in the light.

HOW THE LOST LIGHT AFFECTS SEX

Now what's the connection between sex and this exchange of the glory of God for images? This is what Paul turns to next. Four times in verses 23-28 he says that this exchange of God's glory for other things—this preferring of human glories over God's glory—is the root of disordered sexuality:

> 23 [They] exchanged the glory of the immortal God for images resembling mortal man and birds and animals and creeping things.

> 24 Therefore God gave them up in the lusts of their hearts to impurity, to the dishonoring of their bodies among themselves, 25 because they exchanged the truth about God for a lie and worshiped and served the creature rather than the Creator, who is blessed forever! Amen.

> 26 For this reason God gave them up to dishonorable passions. For their women exchanged natural relations for those that are contrary to nature; 27 and the men likewise gave up natural relations with women and were consumed with passion for

one another, men committing shameless acts with men and receiving in themselves the due penalty for their error.

[28] And since they did not see fit to acknowledge God, God gave them up to a debased mind to do what ought not to be done.

In one sense, the fact that Paul is talking about a same-sex disorientation is incidental. The same dynamics are going to hold true for all distortions of our sexuality. We will note in a moment why Paul focuses explicitly on homosexuality. But our focus is wider.

First, note the connection between verses 23 and 24: They "exchanged the glory of the immortal God for images ... *Therefore* God gave them up in the lusts of their hearts to impurity, to the dishonoring of their bodies among themselves." The word "therefore" is decisive. It means that the vertical dishonoring of God ("[they] exchanged the glory of God") gives rise to (results in, leads to) the horizontal dishonoring of the human body in the disordered sexual desires of their hearts: "God gave them up ... to the dishonoring of their bodies." Humans exchanged God's glory; therefore, they dishonored their bodies.

Second, note the connection between verses 24 and 25:

"God gave them up in the lusts of their hearts to impurity, to the dishonoring of their bodies among themselves, *because* they exchanged the truth about God for a lie and worshiped and served the creature rather than the Creator, who is blessed forever! Amen." Here Paul makes the same point in reverse. Instead of giving the outcome of exchanging God's glory, he gives the cause of dishonoring the body in lusts. The cause of the lust and impurity and dishonoring of the body is that they embraced the lie, the darkness, that the glory of God is less satisfying than something else. They dishonored their bodies because they preferred the creature over the Creator.

Third, note the relationship between verses 25 and 26: "They exchanged the truth about God for a lie ... *For this reason* God gave them up to dishonorable passions." Paul makes the same point for the third time. The reason for their dishonorable passions was that they exchanged the true glory of God for the lie that he is not more desirable than anything.

And fourth, once more Paul says it again. Note the relationship between the two halves of verse 28: "And *since* they did not see fit to acknowledge God [literally: "did not approve of having God in their knowledge"], God gave them up to a debased mind to do what ought not to be done." They did not want God as the dominant reality in their minds. They did not want the glory of God as the supreme value in their hearts. Since they didn't, "therefore" they embraced sexual sin.

Could Paul have made it any clearer that the root problem in sexual sin is that we don't love the light and beauty of the glory of God above all things? We love the man-made image, not the divine reality. We love the lie, not the truth. We love the darkness, not the light. And the fallout for our sexuality is profoundly distorting.

The reason homosexuality is the focus here is probably because it gives the clearest illustration of how the exchange of the beauty we were made for vertically is reflected in the exchange of the beauty we were made for horizontally—in man exchanging woman for man and woman exchanging man for woman. In other words, an unnatural exchange vertically reverberates in unnatural exchanges horizontally.

This is exactly what Paul draws attention to in the way he uses the word "exchanged" through the text. First, he uses the word "exchange" for how we prefer the creature over the Creator. We "exchanged the glory of the immortal God for images ... [We] exchanged the truth about God for a lie" (v 23, 25). Then he uses the word "exchange" for how men prefer men for sexual partners, and women prefer women: "For their women exchanged natural relations for those that are contrary to nature; and the men likewise gave up natural relations with women" (v 26-27). So same-sex relationships stand as a vivid, enacted parable of the disordered sexuality that stems from a disordered relationship with God—specifically, a relationship in which the glories of creation are preferred to the glory of God.

THE DANGERS OF SEX

This exchange—perhaps most vividly portrayed in same-sex relations—applies to all our sexual sins: adultery—exchanging a spouse for an illicit partner, fornication—exchanging God's call to chastity in singleness for unmarried sex; lust—exchanging purity for pornography. All of them—all of our sexual sinning—is rooted in this: we don't treasure the glory of God as supremely desirable over all things. We let the darkness of the lie persuade us that one illicit pleasure or another is more to be desired than God. In the darkness, we fondle the smooth ebony brooch hanging around our neck—not knowing that in the light we would see it is a cockroach. We think the tarantula is a fuzzy toy. We think the lion is a pet and the sound of the rattlesnake is a castanet. That's what it means to live in the dark, where God is less to be desired than sexual pleasure.

Sexual sin grows in the soil of blindness, darkness, and ignorance about the all-satisfying greatness and beauty of God. That's why Peter said to the churches, "As obedient children, do not be conformed to the passions of your former ignorance" (1 Peter 1 v 14). He is saying, *Once you were ignorant of God's worth and beauty and greatness and sweetness. But now you have been "born again" (v 3, 23), "if indeed you have tasted that the Lord is good" (2 v 3)*. Yes, and once you "taste" of God, the "former ignorance" of the taste of sin no longer controls your passions. The lie of sinful sexual desires is exposed.

Paul made the same point about "former ignorance" in relation to sexual sin. He said, "This is the will of God, your sanctification: that you abstain from sexual immorality; that each one of you know how to control his own body in holiness and honor, not in the passion of lust like the Gentiles who do not know God" (1 Thessalonians 4 v 3-5). In other words, Paul traces the distortion and misuse of sexual desire back to the darkness of the unbelieving mind. They don't know God. That is where we all were: in the dark about the infinite beauty and worth of God.

THEY KNOW AND THEY DON'T KNOW

In talking of our "former ignorance," Peter and Paul are not contradicting Romans 1 v 21, where Paul says, "Although they knew God, they did not honor him as God or give thanks to him." There is both knowledge of God and ignorance of God in the non-Christian mind. The knowledge of God is deep and innate:

> [19] What can be known about God is plain to them, because God has shown it to them. [20] For his invisible attributes, namely, his eternal power and divine nature, have been clearly perceived, ever since the creation of the world, in the things that have been made. So they are without excuse. (1 v 19-20)

But this deep, innate knowledge of God is rejected and suppressed. "By their unrighteousness [they] suppress the truth" (v 18). "They did not approve of having God in their knowledge" (v 28). So there is real ignorance of God as well as real knowledge. The knowledge is suppressed and inoperative. The ignorance is desired and powerful. Both Peter and Paul trace the distortions and enslavements of sexual desire back to this ignorance of God—back to the exchange of the glory of God for images. The human soul was made to be satisfied by the glory of

God. When the light of that glory is suppressed, the soul will destroy itself trying to find satisfaction in the deadly darkness.

And it is indeed deadly, as Jesus and the apostles tell us over and over again. Here is where we see the dangerous outcomes of the effects of not living in the light. These warnings are not limited to one or two authors in the New Testament. Jesus, Peter, Paul, John and the writer to the Hebrews all sound the note of danger that lies ahead for those who do not repent of sexual sin.

Consider some of these warnings.

NO SIN LIKE THIS

Paul penetrates to the depths of the sexual sin of fornication, adultery, and in particular prostitution.

> [15] Do you not know that your bodies are members of Christ? Shall I then take the members of Christ and make them members of a prostitute? Never! [16] Or do you not know that he who is joined to a prostitute becomes one body with her? For, as it is written, "The two will become one flesh." [17] But he who is joined to the Lord becomes one spirit with him. [18] Flee from sexual immorality. Every other sin a person commits is outside the body, but the sexually

immoral person sins against his own body. [19] Or do you not know that your body is a temple of the Holy Spirit within you, whom you have from God? You are not your own, [20] for you were bought with a price. So glorify God in your body.

(1 Corinthians 6 v 15-20)

The Christian is united to Christ. This union involves our body and our spirit. Therefore, illicit sexual unions that do not express our union with Christ will contradict it and drag Christ into the bed of unholy pleasure, and make him a partner in the act. For Paul this was breathtakingly unthinkable—as it should be for us.

You might think this is an entirely different explanation of where sexual sin comes from than the one we have seen so far. Here, you might say, sexual sin comes from failing to see that we are members of Christ, so that we drag Christ down to the level of prostitution. To be sure, there is more to this argument than we have seen so far, but it is not entirely different. Paul is assuming that if you saw and cherished the beauty and worth of Christ, you would not do that. The outrage is based on the purity and preciousness and holiness and glory of Christ.

You can see this at the end of the text when Paul says, "You are not your own, for you were bought with a price. So glorify God in your body" (v 19-20).

God owns you. He bought you with the infinitely valuable blood of Christ. Therefore, when we treat our body as if we had the right to do with it as our impulses demand, we treat the worth of Christ and the glory of God with contempt. This has been the point all along.

There is one especially puzzling part of Paul's text. In verse 18, he argues against fornication like this: "Every other sin a person commits is outside the body, but the sexually immoral person sins against his own body." What does that mean? In all the commentaries I have read over the years, it seems to me that there is no complete consensus, but most would agree that in some way Paul sees sexual relations with anyone but your spouse as uniquely defiling or hurtful to the body. There is no other sin like it, he says. So, for example, Roy Ciampa and Brian Rosner say:

> *Paul is not saying that only porneia [sexual immorality] damages the body, but rather that only porneia establishes a "one-flesh" union that is "against the body." Sexual sin is against the body because, as Fisk states, it is "uniquely body-joining, … [and] uniquely body-defiling." As with so many other compressed expressions in the section, we need to supply something to complete our understanding of Paul's thought. Here we might add that porneia is a sin against the body's "rightful ownership"; the believer's body is under*

> *the authority of Christ the Lord (v 12-15), is a temple of*
> *the Holy Spirit (v 19), and was purchased by God (v 20).[1]*

We can speculate about what sorts of unique damages may come to a person who sins in this way. But what should sober us is that the inspired apostle sees something seriously dangerous about sexual sin. There is no other sin like this.

A FINAL WAR FOR THE SOUL

From the present dangers of sexual sin, we move now to the more general warnings about the ultimate damage that sexual sin may bring. Peter writes, "Beloved, I urge you as sojourners and exiles to abstain from the passions of the flesh, which wage war against your soul" (1 Peter 2 v 11). This would not be limited to sinful sexual passions, but it surely includes them. And the danger is that these passions of the flesh aim at destroying the soul. The outcome of sexual sin, if

---

1 Roy E. Ciampa and Brian S. Rosner, *The First Letter to the Corinthians,* The Pillar New Testament Commentary (Eerdmans, 2010), page 264. Some scholars see the words, "Every sin a person commits is outside the body" (v 18, see ESV footnote) not as Paul's own words, but as a slogan quoted from his adversaries in Corinth, similar to the way he probably quoted his opponents in verses 12 and 13. That may be, but in my opinion the wording of the Greek, with its inclusion of a relative clause (ὃ ἐὰν ποιήσῃ ἄνθρωπος) does not sound like a slogan. In either case, Paul's assertion at the end of verse 18 is that sexual immorality really does sin against the body.

God does not intervene and grant repentance, is the same as what happens to a vanquished enemy in war.

The writer to the Hebrews takes the warning to a new level. "Let marriage be held in honor among all, and let the marriage bed be undefiled, for God will judge the sexually immoral and adulterous" (Hebrews 13 v 4). Paul defines that "judgment" as the wrath of God against those who practice sexual immorality: "Put to death therefore what is earthly in you: sexual immorality, impurity, passion, evil desire, and covetousness, which is idolatry. On account of these the wrath of God is coming" (Colossians 3 v 5-6). Of course, sexual sin is not the only sin that brings the judgment of God, but it is one.

And Paul repeatedly calls out this sin as imperiling the souls of those who practice it. Taking us back to the experiences of Israel in the wilderness on their way to the promised land, he warns us that, "We must not indulge in sexual immorality as some of them did, and twenty-three thousand fell in a single day" (1 Corinthians 10 v 8). Sexual sin leads to judgment—"The Lord is an avenger in all these things" (1 Thessalonians 4 v 3-6).

Paul draws out a specific implication of God's judgment and vengeance against sexual sin by mentioning it in the list of sins that keep someone from entering the kingdom of God. "Now the works of the flesh are evident: sexual immorality, impurity, sensuality … I warn you, as I warned you before, that those who do such things will not inherit the kingdom of God" (Galatians 5 v 19-21). And again:

> [9] Do you not know that the unrighteous will not inherit the kingdom of God? Do not be deceived: neither the sexually immoral, nor idolaters, nor adulterers, nor men who practice homosexuality, [10] nor thieves, nor the greedy, nor drunkards, nor revilers, nor swindlers will inherit the kingdom of God.
>
> (1 Corinthians 6 v 9-10)

The apostle John's way of speaking about this exclusion from the kingdom of God is found in the book of Revelation:

> [14] Blessed are those who wash their robes, so that they may have the right to the tree of life and that they may enter the city by the gates. [15] Outside are the dogs and sorcerers and the sexually immoral and murderers and idolaters, and everyone who loves and practices falsehood. (Revelation 22 v 14-15)

But it is not as though the defilements of sexual sin are irremovable, and that if we have sinned sexually, we cannot be part of God's holy kingdom. The point of verse 14 is that we may be washed and accepted. What does it mean to wash our robes? It is to be someone who has "washed their robes and made them white in the blood of the Lamb" (Revelation 7 v 14). Christ died and shed his scarlet blood so that our scarlet sin-stained garments could be made white:

> Come now, let us reason together, says the LORD: though your sins are like scarlet, they shall be as white as snow; though they are red like crimson, they shall become like wool. (Isaiah 1 v 18)

It is wonderfully encouraging for discouraged sinners that Paul speaks in the same way to those who have lived in every manner of sexual sin: "Such were some of you. But you were washed, you were sanctified, you were justified in the name of the Lord Jesus Christ and by the Spirit of our God" (1 Corinthians 6 v 11).

But this is of no encouragement, if we do not treasure Christ and turn from the preference of sex over God. Without this kind of faith—which embraces Jesus as supreme (Matthew 10 v 37)—his blood will do us no good, and Revelation 22 v 15 will be true of us in the last day: "Outside are ... the sexually immoral."

JESUS' STRONGEST WORDS

What does it mean to be "outside"? No one tells us with stronger words about the dangers of sexual sin than the Lord Jesus:

> [27] You have heard that it was said, "You shall not commit adultery." [28] But I say to you that everyone who looks at a woman with lustful intent has already committed adultery with her in his heart. [29] If your right eye causes you to sin, tear it out and throw it away. For it is better that you lose one of your members than that your whole body be thrown into hell. [30] And if your right hand causes you to sin, cut it off and throw it away. For it is better that you lose one of your members than that your whole body go into hell. (Matthew 5 v 27-30)

The severity of these words—lest you be "thrown into hell"—are an echo of the thunderclap behind Romans 1: "[They] exchanged the glory of the immortal God for images!" (v 23). The threat of hell does not come out of nowhere. It is not a prudish revulsion at the fleshiness of sex—God made sex and so, in itself, it is good. No, this threat is the echo of the outrage that genital stimulation and ephemeral hormonal euphoria is preferred over infinite and eternal glory. "The wrath of God is revealed from heaven ... [because people] exchanged the glory of the immortal God for [created things]" (v 18, 23).

Jesus is aiming to wake us up from the dark and dreary stupor of having such weak feelings about the glory of God that we need to augment them or replace them with lustful thoughts about illicit sexual stimulation. Of course, he is not finding fault with the sexual pleasures of the bride and groom in the Song of Solomon, who revel in each other's bodies. That feasting—whether on food or sex—is "made holy by the word of God and prayer" (1 Timothy 4 v 5). Such pleasures are embraced as gifts from God, and they communicate something of God as they are enjoyed within God's wise and beneficial boundaries. But Jesus is not talking about that kind of sex in Matthew 5 v 27-30. He is talking about desires that take forbidden fruit on the tongue of the imagination and get as much pleasure as possible short of the real thing—about "lustful intent" (v 28).

Of that he warns, "If your right eye causes you to sin, tear it out and throw it away." Notice something odd. Jesus says "right eye." But if you tear out only one of your eyes, you can see the woman (or man, or image) just as well as if you had both eyes.

What does that tell us? It tells us that Jesus is not giving a precise, literal method for killing temptation. What he is doing is telling us how seriously we should make war on our sinfulness. Eternal things are at stake. Do what you must to kill sin so that it does not kill you.

Paul put it like this: "If you live according to the flesh you will die, but if by the Spirit you put to death the deeds of the body, you will live" (Romans 8 v 13). Fight sexual sin (and every other sin) with the same seriousness as tearing out an eye and cutting off a hand. Your life depends on it. Eternally.

JOHN'S MOST VIVID PICTURE

Finally in our overview of New Testament warnings we come to John's most vivid picture, of the lake of fire.

> As for the cowardly, the faithless, the detestable, as
> for murderers, the sexually immoral, sorcerers, idola
> ters, and all liars, their portion will be in the lake that
> burns with fire and sulfur, which is the second death.
>
> (Revelation 21 v 8)

The horror of the image of a "lake of fire" is compounded by its duration: "The smoke of their torment goes up forever and ever, and they have no rest, day or night" (14 v 11). This is perhaps the most vivid picture we have of the final end of those whose "sexual immorality" is not covered by the blood of Jesus. Only "in Christ" are we safe from the lake of fire. As the apostle Peter says, "You were ransomed from the futile ways inherited from your forefathers, not with perishable things such as silver or gold, but with the precious blood of Christ, like that of a lamb without blemish or spot" (1 Peter 1 v 18-19). Faith in Christ conquers the lake of fire: "The one who conquers will not be hurt by the second death" (Revelation 2 v 11).

The warnings of the New Testament about the dangers of sex are not meant to leave us paralyzed in fear. They are meant to open our eyes to the magnitude of the glory of God, the enormity of our sin, the justice of our punishment, the wisdom of flying to Christ, and the superior pleasures at God's right hand. It is a gracious thing that the doctor has told us that our condition is terminal; and even more gracious that he offers us the only remedy that heals the disease of sin, and averts the dreadful outcome. It cost him the life of his Son to provide this. Which is another reason why the warnings are so stark for those who spurn such a priceless gift.

RESTORING THE LIGHT OF THE GLORY OF GOD

Recall that the origin of sexual sin is that we have "exchanged the glory of the immortal God for images" (Romans 1 v 23). This vertical exchange surrounds us with darkness. The glory has vanished. It was meant to thrill us. And we have rejected it. We do not prefer God over all things. One of the created things we replace him with is illicit sexual pleasure. The vividness of sexual images has power because the light of glory has gone out.

Here is how this works. I have a clock on my bedside table. It shines the time on the ceiling. So at night, when I turn my light off, I can see "10:30" in red numbers on my ceiling. It is clear, and it holds my attention—in the dark. But when the sun comes up in the morning, those red numbers vanish completely. In the brightness of the sun, I can only see the ceiling. The red numbers thrive on the darkness. They are only visible in the dark.

So it is with illicit sex. Its vividness and power to lure us into sin increases where the glory of God shines least brightly. When God's glory is revealed and treasured most, the power of sinful sexual attraction is broken. The brightness of the sun makes the brightness of the red lights vanish. So when it comes to our sex lives, the

issue is this: Do we see the glory of God? Do we treasure the glory? Are we deeply content, as Paul says, in
every situation (even when sexual satisfaction is denied)
"because of the surpassing worth of knowing Christ Jesus my Lord" (Philippians 3 v 8)?

To help us overcome the dangers of sex, God has
done more than warn us. "His divine power has granted to us all things that pertain to life and godliness"
(2 Peter 1 v 3). How has he done this? Peter goes on.
He has done it "through the knowledge of him who
called us to his own glory and excellence." God empowers us for godly sexuality—and frees us from ungodly sexuality—"through … knowledge." Knowledge
of what? The God of glory and excellence!

In other words, God steps in and begins to reverse
the exchange of Romans 1. There we exchanged the
glory of God for images, and everything became debased and distorted. Now he is reversing that exchange
"through the knowledge of him who called us to his
own glory and excellence." The reawakening of the
soul to the glory of God is the birth of freedom from
sexual bondage.

And how has God given us this knowledge of God's
glory and excellence? By granting "to us his precious
and very great promises, so that through them you may

become partakers of the divine nature, having escaped from the corruption that is in the world because of sinful desire" (2 Peter 1 v 4). The life-changing knowledge of glory comes through God's promises. He makes promises to us. The promises reveal the glory and the excellence of God, and assure us that we will enjoy them forever as we trust in Christ.

When we embrace these promises of God's glory, we "become partakers of the divine nature." That is, God conforms us to his holy character, through faith in his God-saturated promises. And the result of this transformation into God's likeness is escape "from the corruption that is in the world because of sinful desire." In other words, freedom from the power of sinful desire—including sexual desire—comes through:

1) hearing the promises of God,
2) seeing and knowing the glory of God through those promises,
3) being transformed by what we see into the likeness of God's nature, and therefore
4) escaping the corruption that held us in bondage.

THE DANGERS OF SEX IN SUMMARY

In summary, then, the danger of sex is that because our hearts are naturally disordered vertically and God is not our supreme desire, therefore our sexual desires are disordered horizontally and we prefer illicit pleasures to godly ones. We even prefer them over God himself. The outcome of this desecration of God's beauty and worth is the prospect of terrible punishment under God's judgment. But the apex of the glory of the God of glory is his grace. He has made a way for sexual sins to be forgiven and for defiled lives to be made pure.

He did this in the death and resurrection of Christ. And we know he did it specifically for sexual sinners because Paul lists those sinners: "the sexually immoral … idolaters … adulterers … men who practice homosexuality" (1 Corinthians 6 v 9). And then he says, gloriously, "And such were some of you. But you were washed, you were sanctified, you were justified in the name of the Lord Jesus Christ and by the Spirit of our God" (v 11).

Perhaps this was you. Perhaps this *is* you. In some way, Paul is describing all of us. None of us have a perfect record sexually. It is surely true, as Paul says, that exchanging God's glory for sexual immorality leads to destruction. But it is also true—wonderfully true—that repenting of that immorality leads to forgiveness in Christ and eternity with God. And it leads to a deeper, purer enjoyment of sex as a good gift from God, rather than as a way of rejecting God.

Changing the imagery, we may say this: when the planet of sex, which is itself a good thing, comes into the gravitational pull of an alien star, it is drawn into illicit orbits. The most common alien star is a burning preference for sex over God. Such an exchange of treasures begins to swing the planet of sex toward the center. The light of God's beauty has a powerful gravitational attraction on everything in our lives. Only when the sun of God's all-satisfying glory is the center of the solar system of our lives will sex find its beautiful, holy, happy orbit.

THE WEALTH-DESTROYING DANGERS OF MONEY

What about money? How does the good gift of money—so full of potential for blessing—become destructive? How is it related to the exchange of the glory of God for other things? What happens when it takes control of us?

THE FIRST AND THE LAST COMMANDMENTS

Have you ever pondered the possibility that the first and the last of the Ten Commandments are virtually the same, and function as a kind of enclosure, or bracketing, that makes the other eight commandments in the middle possible?

The first commandment is, "You shall have no other gods before me" (Exodus 20 v 3). "Before me" in what sense? Verse 5 makes it plain: "I the LORD your

God am a jealous God." In other words, *You, Israel, are my wife. If your heart goes after another god, it's like a wife getting into bed with another man. I get angry in my holy jealousy. Your heart, your supreme loyalty, your love, your affection, your devotion, your enjoyment belong supremely to me.*

So when God says, "You shall have no other gods before me," he means, *You shall always have me as supreme in your affections. You shall delight in me more than any suitor that comes along. Nothing shall appeal to you more than I do. Embrace me as your supreme treasure and be content in me.* That's the first commandment.

Then the last of the ten commandments is, "You shall not covet" (v 17). The word for "covet" in Hebrew means simply "desire." So the question in defining what "covet" means is the question: When does desire for something—like money, or what money can buy—become bad desire? When does legitimate desire become covetousness?

My suggestion is this: put the last commandment together with the first, and you get your answer. The first commandment is, *No gods before me. Nothing in your heart should compete with me. Desire me so fully that when you have me, you are content.* And then the tenth commandment is, *Don't covet.* Don't have any illegitimate desires. That is, don't desire anything in a way that would undermine your contentment in God. So covetousness—or wrong desire—is desiring anything in such a way that you lose your contentment in God.

PAUL'S STRONGEST WARNING ABOUT THE DANGERS OF MONEY

Let's test this with Paul's strongest words about money and how money relates to contentment. In 1 Timothy 6 v 5-10, Paul starts with a description of people very much like the people we saw in Romans 1, only now the issue in focus is the disordered craving for money, not the disordered craving for sex. He speaks of people...

> [5] who are depraved in mind and deprived of the truth, imagining that godliness is a means of gain. [6] But godliness with contentment is great gain, [7] for we brought nothing into the world, and we cannot take anything out of the world. [8] But if we have food and clothing, with these we will be content. [9] But those who desire to be rich fall into temptation, into a snare, into many senseless and harmful desires that plunge people into ruin and destruction. [10] For the love of money is a root of all kinds of evils. It is through this craving that some have wandered away from the faith and pierced themselves with many pangs.

It is clear that money is dangerous. I know it's not the money itself that destroys the soul. It's the craving. The desiring. As the nineteenth-century Scottish minister George Macdonald said:

> *It is not the rich man only who is under the dominion of things; they too are slaves who, having no money, are unhappy for the lack of it.*[2]

Nevertheless, Jesus did say, "Only with difficulty will a rich person enter the kingdom of heaven" (Matthew 19 v 23). He didn't just say it is hard for any person who *loves money* to get into heaven, but for any person who is *rich*. He said, in effect, that money itself is dangerous—not evil, just dangerous—because of how quickly and easily we can be deceived by it. Jesus says, "The deceitfulness of riches choke the word" (Matthew 13 v 22). Money is dangerous because it has such a power to deceive. It's a good liar.

Handling money is like handling a live wire that can electrocute you. That's the gist of Paul's words to Timothy: "Those who desire to be rich fall into temptation, into a snare, into many senseless and harmful desires that plunge people into ruin and de-

---

2 *George Macdonald: An Anthology,* ed. C.S. Lewis (The Centenary Press, 1946), page 45

struction. For the love of money is a root of all kinds of evils. It is through this craving that some have wandered away from the faith and pierced themselves with many pangs" (1 Timothy 5 v 9-10). That is very strong language. "Temptation ... snare ... many senseless and harmful desires that plunge people into ruin and destruction ... pierced themselves with many pangs." Surely Paul means for us to be struck with a profound caution.

GODLINESS WITH CONTENTMENT IS GREAT GAIN

Over the years, it has struck me—in view of Jesus' warning that riches make it hard for people to get into heaven and Paul's warning that those who desire to be rich plunge into ruin and destruction—how strange it is how many Christian people still pursue wealth. It's as though they either do not believe him, or they think they will be the exception to the rule, or they just don't think God's word could mean what it says.

But Paul means what he says—desiring to be rich is deadly. And there is more. The key that unlocks this text is in verse 6: "Godliness with contentment is great gain." What is the protection against these deadly effects of money? Answer: a heart that is content in God. Are you deeply satisfied in God, so that this satisfaction, this contentment, doesn't collapse when God ordains that you have much or little? Having little can destroy contentment in God by making us feel he is stingy or uncaring or powerless. And having much can destroy our contentment in God by making us feel that God is superfluous, or quite secondary as a helper and treasure.

It is no small thing to learn in life how not to lose our contentment in God. This is what life is for—living to show that God is all-glorious. And this is shown, among other ways, by how he is gloriously sufficient to give us contentment in himself in the best and worst of times. Paul had learned the secret of how to do that:

> [11] I have learned in whatever situation I am to be content. [12] I know how to be brought low, and I know how to abound. In any and every circumstance, I have learned the secret of facing plenty and hunger, abundance and need. [13] I can do all things through him who strengthens me. (Philippians 4 v 11-13)

Paul had learned "to be content." This is the key to the right use of money in 1 Timothy 6 v 5-10. Paul said he had learned the secret of this contentment. "I have learned the secret of facing plenty and hunger, abundance and need" (Philippians 4 v 12). What was the secret? I think he gives the secret in the previous chapter of Philippians: "I count everything as loss because of the surpassing worth of knowing Christ Jesus my Lord" (3 v 8).

In other words, to put it in modern terms, when the stock market goes up or he gets a bonus, he says, *I find Jesus more precious and valuable and satisfying than my increasing money.* And when the stock market goes down or he faces a pay cut, he says, *I find Jesus more precious and valuable and satisfying than all that I have lost.* The glory and beauty and worth and preciousness of Christ is the secret of contentment that keeps money from controlling him.

MONEY FAILS WHEN YOU NEED IT MOST

There is another sad truth about money in Paul's strong word in 1 Timothy 6. In verse 7, Paul makes plain that money will let you down just when you need the most help—when you are dying. "We brought nothing into the world, and we cannot take anything out of the world." Just at the moment when you need heavenly riches—"treasures in heaven"—money walks away from you. It abandons you. It will not go with you to help you. And nothing that you bought with it can go either. You are thrown back entirely on another reality.

Jesus pleaded with us not to think that laying up money on earth would be of any use as we enter the world to come.

> [19] Do not lay up for yourselves treasures on earth, where moth and rust destroy and where thieves break in and steal, [20] but lay up for yourselves treasures in heaven, where neither moth nor rust destroys and where thieves do not break in and steal. [21] For where your treasure is, there your heart will be also.
>
> (Matthew 6 v 19-21)

What an utter folly to devote your life to amassing riches—or to want to. Wealth will be of no help in the end. Jesus felt so strongly about this warning that he told a parable to drive it home:

> [16] The land of a rich man produced plentifully, [17] and he thought to himself, "What shall I do, for I have nowhere to store my crops?" [18] And he said, "I will do this: I will tear down my barns and build larger ones, and there I will store all my grain and my goods. [19] And I will say to my soul, 'Soul, you have ample goods laid up for many years; relax, eat, drink, be merry.'" [20] But God said to him, "Fool! This night your soul is required of you, and the things you have prepared, whose will they be?" [21] So is the one who

lays up treasure for himself and is not rich toward
God. (Luke 12 v 16-21)

Fool! Whose will all this be when you are dead? Money
is no friend in death.

MONEY FAILS YOU EVEN BEFORE THE END

But it is not just that money will let you down in the
end. It lets you down before the end. "He who loves
money will not be satisfied with money, nor he who
loves wealth with his income; this also is vanity" (Ec-
clesiastes 5 v 10). Money does not satisfy now. I know
many will say, "Oh yes it does. My money is a good
friend. It does not let me down. I have a great house,
and two cars, and a fine private school for my kids, and
a boat, and a cabin, and lots of life insurance, and pen-
sions and annuities. It may not go with me to the other
world—if there is another world—but it definitely has
not let me down here!"

Really?

I will place my bet with the Preacher of Ecclesi-
astes. You were made for satisfaction with God, and
your money is blinding you to that. There are deep
longings that you have. They rise up in the night.
They creep up on you when you are alone and discouraged. If you are honest, you know the stuff you

have surrounded yourself with cannot touch the deepest longings of your heart. You were not made to be satisfied with stuff. And none of that stuff can still the fears, and the onrush, of aging and death. No, you are kidding yourself. The word is true: "He who loves money will not be satisfied with money."

George Macdonald penetrated to the reason that our elusive quest to find happiness in having stuff does not work:

> *The heart of man cannot hoard. His brain or his hand may gather into its box and hoard, but the moment the thing has passed into the box, the heart has lost it and is hungry again. If a man would have, it is the Giver he must have … Therefore all that he makes must be free to come and go through the heart of his child; he can enjoy it only as it passes, can enjoy only its life, its soul, its vision, its meaning, not itself.*[3]

There is no link between having much money and knowing much happiness in this life—or the next. When the biblical wise man says, "Better is…" he means, "More deep contentment is…"

> "Better is the little that the righteous has than the abundance of many wicked." (Psalm 37 v 16)

....

3 *George Macdonald: An Anthology,* page 106

"Better is a little with the fear of the LORD than great treasure and trouble with it." (Proverbs 15 v 16)

"Better is a dinner of herbs where love is than a fattened ox and hatred with it." (Proverbs 15 v 17)

"Better is a little with righteousness than great revenues with injustice." (Proverbs 16 v 8)

"Better is a dry morsel with quiet than a house full of feasting with strife." (Proverbs 17 v 1)

"Better is a poor person who walks in his integrity than one who is crooked in speech and is a fool." (Proverbs 19 v 1)

"Better is a poor man who walks in his integrity than a rich man who is crooked in his ways." (Proverbs 28 v 6)

In other words, the key to happiness in this life is not wealth. You cannot find happiness in something that blinds you to the true source of happiness. Jesus repeatedly portrayed himself and his promises and his kingdom—now and forever—as a relationship and a hope and a place of supreme happiness. What kept people from seeing this? Here is one of his graphic answers:

[16] [Jesus said,] "A man once gave a great banquet and invited many. [17] And at the time for the banquet he sent his servant to say to those who had been invited, 'Come, for everything is now ready.' [18] But they all alike began to make excuses. The first said to him, 'I have bought a field, and I must go out and see it. Please have me excused.' [19] And another said, 'I have bought five yoke of oxen, and I go to examine them. Please have me excused.' [20] And another said, 'I have married a wife, and therefore I cannot come.' [21] So the servant came and reported these things to his master. Then the master of the house became angry and said to his servant, 'Go out quickly to the streets and lanes of the city, and bring in the poor and crippled and blind and lame.' [22] And the servant said, 'Sir, what you commanded has been done, and still there is room.' [23] And the master said to the servant, 'Go out to the highways and hedges and compel people to come in, that my house may be filled. [24] For I tell you, none of those men who were invited shall taste my banquet.'"

(Luke 14 v 16-24)

Two out of the three excuses which these people give for not coming to the banquet of everlasting joy are money-related: I bought. I bought. "I have bought a field," so I prefer to "go out and see it" than to come to the all-satisfying banquet of the kingdom of God. "I have bought five yoke of oxen," so I prefer to "go to examine them" than to come to the all-satisfying banquet of the kingdom of God.

Who of us has not tasted the power of this illusion? Shopping at the mall. Surfing for a purchase online. Checking the stock-market quotes. Who has not felt the pull of the power to have stuff, to buy, to own? It is very deep, and very dangerous. It blinds someone to what is truly beautiful and truly desirable and truly satisfying. It substitutes a dollar bill for the divine. God may send his messenger to us with a word of truth, a word of light, but for many, Jesus says, "The deceitfulness of riches choke the word, and it proves unfruitful" (Matthew 13 v 22). Riches choke. What is "choke" but another image of the blinding—and suffocating—effect of riches as they deceive us into thinking that having stuff is more satisfying than the light of God's word?

MONEY MAKES YOU HARMFUL

Not only does money disappoint and deceive and suffocate us; it also has the power to make us harmful to others, not just ourselves. This too is a great danger of money. Luke said of the most influential class of religious leaders in Jesus' day that they were lovers of money: "the Pharisees, who were lovers of money, heard all these things, and they ridiculed [Jesus]" (Luke 16 v 14). And this love of money turned them into greedy graspers. That's my translation of the Greek word *harpages* (ἁρπαγῆς) in Luke 11 v 39-40:

> [39] And the Lord said to him, "Now you Pharisees cleanse the outside of the cup and of the dish, but inside you are full of greed [ἁρπαγῆς] and wickedness. [40] You fools! Did not he who made the outside make the inside also?"

Harpages (ἁρπαγῆς) is not your ordinary word for greed and covetousness (that is *pleonexia*, πλεονεξία). This is grasping—and grasping usually involves seeking to take what belongs to someone else. It's the kind of greed that causes the scribes to "devour widows' houses and for a pretense make long prayers" (Luke 20 v 47). So the religious precision and legalism of the Pharisees were not the root of the Pharisees' problem. Those were cover-ups for the love of money. And this love of money made the Pharisees cruel to people, even devouring widows' houses.

Jesus told a parable to illustrate the way in which riches blind us to the needs of the poor and make us callous and indifferent, even to the needs close at hand:

> [19] There was a rich man who was clothed in purple and fine linen and who feasted sumptuously every day. [20] And at his gate was laid a poor man named Lazarus, covered with sores, [21] who desired to be fed with what fell from the rich man's table. Moreover, even the dogs came and licked his sores. [22] The poor man died and was carried by the angels to Abraham's side. The rich man also died and was buried, [23] and in Hades, being in torment, he lifted up his eyes and saw Abraham far off and Lazarus at his side. [24] And he called out, "Father Abraham, have mercy on me, and send Lazarus to dip the end of his finger in water and cool my tongue, for I am in anguish in this flame." [25] But Abraham said, "Child, remember that you in your lifetime received your good things, and Lazarus in like manner bad things; but now he is comforted here, and you are in anguish."
>
> (Luke 16 v 19-25)

One of the main lessons Jesus draws out of this parable is in verse 25—the rich and indifferent have their party in this world; the poor and faithful have their party in the next. And what makes that partying so flagrant— "he feasted sumptuously every day"—is that Lazarus was "at his gate." He only wanted crumbs from the rich man's table—but the dogs gave him more attention.

This is what riches can do to the human soul. It not only can lead to the ruin of our happiness, but can also make us cruel and heartless to others on our way to our own ruin—the rich ignoring the nearby poor; the money-loving, workaholic father neglecting his children; the mercenary soldier who cares nothing for his comrades; the wolf in sheep's clothing who poses as a pastor to fleece the flock; the pimp who wants his pay while turning girls into prostitutes. The ruinous effects of riches are endless.

MEGAN'S CONFESSION AND QUESTION

Just as I was putting the final touches on this manuscript to send it off to the publisher, I did a recording session for the podcast Ask Pastor John. One of the questions that I was asked was from a woman named Megan. She wrote:

> Pastor John, I have a confession: I love stuff, and I am very materialistic. I buy things online and get a thrill in buying as well as getting things in the mail. I know I need to stop this, and I want to stop. But how do I? And why do I do it in the first place?

Here is what I said to Megan in this recording:[4]

I have tasted enough of what you are talking about,
Megan, that I think I can speak with some sense of
empathy, even though for me, the temptation is almost
entirely restricted to books. I love to look at books online. It gives me pleasure to click on the purchase of
a book. And when the box shows up in the mail, I'm
sure I feel some of the same pleasure that you are talking about. So I have to guard my soul here. These are
very treacherous waters we are swimming in.

Why is it that we get this kind of pleasure from ordering things—things!—that we can hold in our hands—
and why is it that our pleasure rises when those things
come in the mail?

As I have tried to analyze my own heart, and read
about the experience of others, and look at the way
things are marketed to us, it seems to me that the
pleasure arises mainly from the elusive sense that buy-
ing and receiving things is life-giving, or provides a
sense of empowerment.

When a book arrives, for example, there is the amor-
phous, euphoric sense that life will be better for me.

4 Audio available at desiringgod.org/interviews/by-series/ask-pastor-john

My knowledge will be larger. My influence will be greater. Some of my weakness and limitation of ignorance will be overcome. In other words, there's a sense that somehow my life will go better, and I will be a stronger, capable person.

And, of course, for someone else, it may not be books but clothing or tools or technical gadgets. And in their case, then, the sense of life-giving empowerment would be that they would somehow now look better or be more productive or be more cool with the most up-to-date device.

And we should admit that to some degree there is truth in that: we may indeed be enhanced in some way to be more productive or fruitful in a good way, not just a bad way. But if we are honest—and it seems like Megan is being honest—the pleasures we feel are largely not noble. They're not coming primarily from the fact that we are being equipped as better servants of Christ.

So we need to hear the words of Jesus: "Take care, and be on your guard against all covetousness, for one's life does not consist in the abundance of his possessions" (Luke 12 v 15). That strikes right at the heart of the matter—life does not consist in the abundance of possessions. That feeling that the arrival of packages in the

mail is wonderfully life-giving is an illusion. The euphoria is short-lived and shallow. It keeps us from the deeper pleasures for which we were made.

A second reason why I think we are so hungry for this
kind of elusive life-giving empowerment of the arrival
of packages is that there is at least a partial void, and
emptiness, in our hearts that is meant to be satisfied
by Jesus—his fellowship and his ministry. Paul said in
Philippians 4 that he had learned the secret of contentment: namely, how to have much and how to have
little. In other words, his happiness was not in having.

And the key seems to be what Paul said back in Philippians 3 v 8: namely, that he counted everything as loss
because of the surpassing value of knowing Christ Jesus. When we are not content in Christ to that degree,
there will be a craving in our hearts that very naturally
tries to feed off of the sense of life-giving in the sense
of empowerment that comes through stuff. So you
and I, Megan, need to devote ourselves to feeding our
hearts on Christ and his word.

But not just his word and his fellowship but also his
way of life. I'm thinking now of Acts 20 v 35, where
we're told Jesus said it is more blessed to give than
to receive. The fact that we get more pleasure out of

receiving than giving shows that something has gone wrong in our hearts—because we were designed, as followers of Christ, to experience even greater euphoria in giving. Perhaps this pleasure has fallen into disuse for you, Megan, and to recover it would free you from the lesser pleasures of materialism.

Maybe the very best thing I could say, because it is so breathtaking and so influential and powerful when it really grips us, is what Paul says in first Corinthians 3 v 21-23: "Let no one boast in men. For all things are yours, whether Paul or Apollos or Cephas or the world or life or death or the present or the future—all are yours, and you are Christ's, and Christ is God's."

Megan, if you are a Christian, you already possess all material things. You really do! Your Father created and owns everything. As his child you will inherit it, and it will all be at your disposal in the age to come in the new heavens and the new earth. This is why Jesus said not to lay up treasures on earth but in heaven. In heaven we will have them forever, and for the first time we will be fit to use them without greed and without idolatry. So in a sense, abundance of material things can wait. We have more important things to do now: love God, love people, and find the greatest pleasure in giving.

SUMMARY AND REMEDY FOR THE DANGERS OF MONEY

Given the frequency with which the Scriptures speak of the dangers of money, it is fair to say that here we have only scratched the surface. But that scratch is sobering. Money is a great deceiver (Mark 4 v 19). It can deceive us into thinking and feeling that what we can buy is more satisfying than God. Few things lure us to exchange the glory of God more readily than money does. Money wakens desire for what it can buy; this desire becomes covetousness, competing with God; this covetousness destroys our contentment in the glory of God; and contrary to the first and second commandments, we thus become idolaters—people who prefer anything over God. Paul says in Colossians 3 v 5, "Put to death ... covetousness, which is idolatry."

One of the greatest motivations for not loving money or for trying to overcome our fears with money is found in Hebrews 13 v 5-6:

> [5] Keep your life free from love of money, and be content with what you have, for he has said, "I will never leave you nor forsake you." [6] So we can confidently say, "The Lord is my helper; I will not fear; what can man do to me?"

Notice that the writer to the Hebrews *argues*. That is, he gives reasons. He gives grounds for freedom from the love of money. *Be free from the love of money and be content,* he says, *because God has promised something.* So the power of the love of money is to be broken by God's promise to be something for us. What is that? "Be free … because God has promised, 'I will never leave you nor forsake you.'" In other words, if you enjoy the presence of God more than the presence of money, you will be freed by the promise of his presence. Liberty from the satisfaction of money's presence comes from the superior satisfaction of God's presence. That is how you put covetousness "to death." You kill it with the sword of God's word, which promises more of God.

The argument goes on. In verse 6, the writer says, "so," or "therefore." Therefore, what? Therefore, we can say with deep confidence, "The Lord is my helper; I will not fear; what can man do to me?" Because of the promise of God's glorious presence ("I will never leave you"), therefore, the fears that are making me crave money are overcome. God, not money, is now my refuge. God, not money, is now my sweet safety and comfort and peace.

The sun of God's glory is now the massive center, and by its gravitational pull the planet of money begins to find its true orbit of service in our lives—an orbit that we will trace in more detail in the last chapter.

THE SELF-DESTROYING
DANGERS OF POWER

We defined power as the capacity to get what you want, or the capacity to pursue what you value. We tend to admire this capacity. It is part of what glory is.

So the glory of athletes is their power to rise above all competitors and be the strongest—the best. The glory of scholars is the power of their intellect— their memory, analytical precision, comprehensive ability to synthesize and wisdom to draw out profound truths. The glory of an actor or actress is their power to render a character so as to rivet attention and draw acclamation. The glory of politicians is their power to persuade and move a bill, over all opposition, into legislation. The glory of a teacher is the power to explain with clarity and winsomeness so that understanding is increased and excitement is stirred in the students.

WHAT POWER PURSUES

We admire this capacity to pursue a value when the value pursued is good. When great power is wielded in the pursuit of great good, we stand amazed and rejoice. God has appointed human government, for example, to wield power for good. "Be subject for the Lord's sake to every human institution, whether it be to the emperor as supreme, or to governors as sent by him to punish those who do evil and to praise those who do good" (1 Peter 2 v 13-14). When power is wielded to do justice, we rejoice.

But there is another side to power: "When the wicked rule, the people groan" (Proverbs 29 v 2). Power may pursue great good, but it may also pursue great evil. When Rehoboam became king of Israel, he told the people, "My father made your yoke heavy, but I will add to your yoke. My father disciplined you with whips, but I will discipline you with scorpions" (1 Kings 12 v 14). When Laban, Isaac's brother-in-law, saw that Jacob was running away with his daughter, he warned him, "It is in my power to do you harm" (Genesis 31 v 29).

And therein lies one of the dangers of power. Morally, it is no better than the goal it pursues. It is a "good" only in the way that a saw is good—and one can use a saw to cut firewood but also to deface an heirloom. In our best moments, what we love to see is great power in the pursuit of great ends.

SELF-EXALTATION THROUGH POWER

Not only is power dangerous because it can be used to bring about evil, but also because it can be used to exalt the one who has it. Since all humans admire glory, and power can be part of glory, we are all tempted to seek this admiration by getting this power. We love to be admired and praised, and so we bend what power we have toward getting applause. In other words, our power is employed to exalt ourselves. This is a great danger.

In fact, for many, this craving for attention and admiration may be deeper than the desire for sex or money. These things are not easy to untangle. Jeremiah cries out, "The heart is deceitful above all things, and desperately sick; who can understand it?" (Jeremiah 17 v 9). Indeed, who can? As David says, "Who can discern his errors?" (Psalm 19 v 12).

In sexual exploits, is a woman craving a man's touch, or the display of her own seductive power? Is a man craving titillation, or admiration? Surely, these are so entangled as to be inseparable—in one person, sensual pleasure is rising to the top; in another person, ego-satisfaction is rising to the top. The lust for power and sex are indivisible.

This indivisibility is even more obvious in the case of money and power. People with the capacity to get wealth are not just tempted to gather money, but to gather the emblems of wealth. Few wealthy people hide their wealth. They wear their wealth. They drive their wealth. They live in their wealth. They sit in the chairs that only their wealth can afford. Their neighborhood declares their wealth. Their airline class declares their wealth. Their hotel declares their wealth.

For most people, money would lose half its pleasure if no one knew they had it. Money says, *I am powerful. I have great capacity to get wealth. I have the power of intellect to outsmart my competitors. Admire my work ethic, my ingenuity, my timing, my shrewdness, my relational savvy, my courage to take the perfect risk. I am not wealthy for no reason. I am wealthy because I have the roots of power within me.*

Jesus dealt with this danger among his apostles repeatedly. In the Gospel of Mark, the depth of the human craving for power and position becomes painfully clear. Three times on the way to Jerusalem, where he will die, Jesus foretells his death, only to be met with the utterly oblivious craving for power in his disciples, as if they did not have a clue that to be a disciple of Jesus was to deny yourself and take up your cross and be shamed and die with him. What they could not grasp was that following Christ means death, not power.

THREE WARNINGS

First, in Mark 8 v 31-32, "[Jesus] began to teach them that the Son of Man must suffer many things and be rejected by the elders and the chief priests and the scribes and be killed, and after three days rise again. And he said this plainly." Years later, Peter would say that Christ was "leaving you an example, so that you might follow in his steps" (1 Peter 2 v 21).

But what did Peter say at the time, in Mark 8? "Peter took him aside and began to rebuke him" (Mark 8 v 32). In other words, *I will not let that happen to you. I will use my strength to protect you, and we will stand against our enemies and defeat them, and you will not be shamed. You will be enthroned.* It was well meant—but full of misguided pride and power.

So Jesus turned and "rebuked Peter and said, 'Get behind me, Satan! For you are not setting your mind on the things of God, but on the things of man.' And calling the crowd to him with his disciples, he said to them, 'If anyone would come after me, let him deny himself and take up his cross and follow me'" (v 33-34). Jesus had prophesied his coming weakness and death. Peter responded in power. And Jesus called it satanic. "Get behind me, Satan!"

Second, in Mark 9, they were passing through Galilee. "He was teaching his disciples, saying to them, 'The Son of Man is going to be delivered into the hands of men, and they will kill him. And when he is killed, after three days he will rise'" (Mark 9 v 31). Mark comments, "But they did not understand" (v 32).

Then, a while later, Jesus asked what they were talking about on the way. At least they had the grace to feel some shame: "They kept silent, for on the way they had argued with one another about who was the greatest" (v 34). Picture the painful disconnect for Jesus. He had just said for the second time that he was going up to Jerusalem to be rejected and die. The next thing his followers did was argue about which of them was the greatest—who would have the most powerful position in the kingdom. They were not stunned at the self-sacrificing love of Jesus. They were consumed with themselves—their power.

Patiently, Jesus sat down and taught them: "'If anyone would be first, he must be last of all and servant of all.' And he took a child and put him in the midst of them, and taking him in his arms, he said to them, 'Whoever receives one such child in my name receives me, and whoever receives me, receives not me but him who sent me'" (v 35-37). These are astonishing words. They don't just indict the glory-hungry, power-craving attitude of the disciples. They also explain that the path of lowliness (caring for a child who can offer no reward or renown) is the way to "receive Christ" and "receive God." "Whoever receives one such child in my name receives me, and whoever receives me, receives not me but him who sent me."

This is the great remedy for the disease of power-craving. As Jesus shows his incomparable, self-sacrificing love by going to the cross of Calvary, instead of being consumed with a conversation about your own greatness, be amazed at his greatness. If we were stunned by and satisfied with Christ, our craving for self-exalting power would be broken. We would be set free from the universal human sickness of self-centeredness.

The third warning, in Mark 10, again comes as "they were on the road, going up to Jerusalem" (Mark

10 v 32). The atmosphere was tense. "They were ... afraid." Once more Jesus said, "See, we are going up to Jerusalem, and the Son of Man will be delivered over to the chief priests and the scribes, and they will condemn him to death and deliver him over to the Gentiles. And they will mock him and spit on him, and flog him and kill him. And after three days he will rise" (v 33-34).

This time, there is no lapse in time. Immediately, and shockingly, "James and John, the sons of Zebedee, came up to him and said to him, 'Teacher, we want you to do for us whatever we ask of you.' And he said to them, 'What do you want me to do for you?' And they said to him, 'Grant us to sit, one at your right hand and one at your left, in your glory'" (v 35-37). He had just said, *They will mock me and spit on me and flog me and kill me.* And their first thought was which of them might have the place of greatest glory—greatest power.

Understandably, "when the ten heard it, they began to be indignant at James and John" (v 41). So Jesus, again with magnificent patience, taught them.

> [42] You know that those who are considered rulers of the Gentiles lord it over them, and their great ones exercise authority over them. [43] But it shall not be so among you. [44] But whoever would be great among

> you must be your servant, and whoever would be
> first among you must be slave of all. [45] For even the
> Son of Man came not to be served but to serve, and
> to give his life as a ransom for many. (v 42-45)

One of the greatest aspects of the glory of Christ is
that he walked through the valley of lowliness and suffering and sacrifice and ignominy on the way to the
mountain of exaltation. This is why the Son of Man
came. To serve. To give his life. This is why the Father
raised him and gave him great glory.

> [7] [He] emptied himself, by taking the form of a serv-
> ant, being born in the likeness of men. [8] And being
> found in human form, he humbled himself by be-
> coming obedient to the point of death, even death
> on a cross. [9] Therefore God has highly exalted him
> and bestowed on him the name that is above every
> name. (Philippians 2 v 7-9)

First comes weakness and sacrifice and suffering and
death. Then comes glory. This is what Jesus was teaching and showing. You can't turn it around. God will not
allow it. "Whoever exalts himself will be humbled, and
whoever humbles himself will be exalted" (Matthew
23 v 12). We will see it more prominently in the next
chapter, but here it should be noted: Jesus is telling the

disciples that power is given for serving others. The greatest power is in humility and service. Power comes from God by renouncing power in ourselves, and praise comes from God as we renounce the pursuit of praise from others.

WHY DO WE CRAVE SELF-EXALTATION?

So the greatest danger of power is craving it in order to exalt ourselves. Why do we do that? Why is this a universal human trait? It may show itself in a thousand varieties of subtle expression or blatant expression, but it is universal. We are all selfish. We all want to be exalted, even if we manifest it in the seeming weakness of self-pity. Years ago in my book *Desiring God*, I put it like this:

> The nature and depth of human pride are illuminated by comparing boasting with self-pity. Both are manifestations of pride. Boasting is the response of pride to success. Self-pity is the response of pride to suffering. Boasting says, "I deserve admiration because I have achieved so much." Self-pity says, "I deserve admiration because I have sacrificed so much." Boasting is the voice of pride in the heart of the strong. Self-pity is the voice of pride in the heart of the weak. Boasting sounds self-sufficient. Self-pity sounds self-sacrificing.

The reason self-pity does not look like pride is that it appears to be needy. But the need arises from a wounded ego, and the desire of the self-pitying is not really for others to see them as helpless, but as heroes. The need self-pity feels does not come from a sense of unworthiness, but from a sense of unrecognized worthiness. It is the response of unapplauded pride.[5]

Our love of praise and power (and, if necessary, pity) is insidious and deceptive. It is indiscriminate about the praising audience. We crave to be made much of, whether from a band of fellow thieves, or from a church congregation, or from a father, or from our children, or our colleagues, or teammates, or boyfriend.

Why do all humans have this craving? Because we have all exchanged the glory of God for images (Romans 1 v 23)—especially the one in the mirror. The reason we abuse power is because we do not delight in the glory of God's right to all power. When we are blind to the glory of God's passion to be known and loved as the source and sum of all power, we take it for our own, and use it for ourselves. That is not why God created the universe—or us.

....

5 John Piper, *Desiring God: Meditations of a Christian Hedonist,* Revised Edition (Multnomah, 2011), page 302

GOD'S AIMS TO SHOW HIS POWER

God created the universe and he governs the universe in order to put the supremacy of his all-sustaining, all-providing, all-controlling power on display for our admiration and trust and pleasure. He means for it to be known. And he means for nobody, anywhere, at any time to claim any power that is not God's power. We do not like this truth and disapprove of having it in our knowledge (Romans 1 v 28). But there it is. And it is good news, even if it assaults our craving to be God. It is good news because we are wired so that, in our best moments even as fallen sinners, we love to see power on display in the cause of a great purpose. Admiration of greatness—including great power—is a great pleasure. So when we look at the following texts about God's exaltation of his power, we should be aware that this is for his glory and our joy.

- Exodus 14 v 4: "I will harden Pharaoh's heart, and he will pursue them, and I will get glory over Pharaoh and all his host, and the Egyptians shall know that I am the LORD."

- Judges 7 v 2: "The LORD said to Gideon, 'The people with you are too many for me to give the Midianites into their hand, lest Israel boast over me, saying, "My own hand has saved me."'"

- Jeremiah 16 v 21: "Behold … I will make them know my power and my might, and they shall know that my name is the LORD."
- John 19 v 10-11: "Pilate said to [Jesus], '… Do you not know that I have authority to release you and authority to crucify you?' Jesus answered him, 'You would have no authority over me at all unless it had been given you from above.'"
- Romans 9 v 17: "For this very purpose I raised you [Pharaoh] up, that I might show my power in you."
- Romans 9 v 22: "What if God, desiring … to make known his power, has endured with much patience vessels of wrath prepared for destruction?"
- 2 Corinthians 4 v 7: "We have this treasure in jars of clay, to show that the surpassing power belongs to God and not to us."
- 2 Corinthians 12 v 9: "My grace is sufficient for you, for my power is made perfect in weakness."

God is the all-glorious God of power. He aims to uphold and display his glory for the dismay of his enemies and the delight of his admiring people. Therefore, the great danger for naturally self-exalting human beings is that we be deceived into thinking that power—any power—is ours by right. It is not ours. It is God's—all of it. And it is on loan to us—in measure—to use for his great purposes:

[17] Beware lest you say in your heart, "My power and the might of my hand have gotten me this wealth." [18] You shall remember the LORD your God, for it is he who gives you power to get wealth.

(Deuteronomy 8 v 17-18)

It is a deadly mistake—literally. It is absolute folly to claim a power for ourselves that belongs only to God. It is, strictly speaking, treason. And that is a capital offense. The reason the pathway away from death to eternal life is the path of faith is because faith admits unworthiness and helplessness. Faith looks away from ourselves to the One who offers grace and power to save us. Holding on to the illusion of self-sufficiency—power to save ourselves—is suicide. Salvation is by faith in the power of another, not ourselves.

The apostle Paul strips fallen man of all pretensions to self-saving power when he says in Romans 8 v 7-8, "The mind that is set on the flesh is hostile to God, for it does not submit to God's law; indeed, it cannot [that is, does not have the power]. Those who are in the flesh cannot please God [they do not have the power]." Paul's view of human nature is that it is so radically opposed to God that it has no power to change that corruption. If we are to be saved, it will be by the exertion of omnipotent divine grace. God must raise us from the dead (Ephesians 2 v 5). He must open the eyes of the blind (2 Corinthians 4 v 6). All the power to save us comes from outside of us. That is why clutching our own pretensions of power is deadly.

THE DOUBLE REMEDY FOR POWER-ADDICTION

The double remedy for this deadly addiction to power is found in 1 Peter 2 v 21. Peter has just told servants to renounce the power of pursuing revenge. He has told them that it is "a gracious thing, when, mindful of God, one endures sorrows while suffering unjustly" (v 19). This looks weak. It is a remarkable refusal to act in self-exalting power. Then Peter says, "For to this you have been called, because Christ also suffered for you, leaving you an example, so that you might follow in his steps" (v 21).

There is a double remedy for power-craving in these words. One is in the words "for you": "Christ ... suffered for you." The other is in the words "leaving you an example."

On the one hand, the sin of our power-craving, and our desire to return evil for evil, must be atoned for, and forgiven. Otherwise, there is no remedy for us. We are lost. This is why the words "suffered for you" are so crucial. Three verses later, Peter illustrates what these words mean: "He himself bore our sins in his body on the tree ... By his wounds you have been healed" (v 24). "Suffered for you" means "bore our sins" in his suffering. This is the magnificent remedy for our guilt: when Christ died "for us," he bore the sin of our power-craving and our desire to return evil for evil. The punishment we deserved, and have no power to escape, fell on him. As we turn from the sin of power-craving to fight for humility and the servant heart of Jesus, we do not fight as condemned people trying to earn approval. We fight as forgiven people trying, in the power of God's Spirit, to become what we are.

The other part of the double remedy for the sin of our power-craving is that, in his suffering, Christ was "leaving [us] an example, so that [we] might follow in his steps." What does it mean, for our cleansed and forgiven souls, to have the Son of God as an example of stunning self-sacrifice on the way to glory?

It means multiple things. The effect of this on us is manifold. First, for example, it stirs our desires to be like him. Second, it assures us that the path of suffering and weakness and sacrifice really does lead to glory. If God raised him and gave him a great name, he will raise us also. Third, and perhaps most important, this example of suffering is an absolutely essential and magnificent part of the beauty of Christ. This is his peculiar glory[6]—that he would condescend from such a height of deity, of power, to such a depth of naked, beaten, mocked, spit-upon, crucified humiliation— that he would do that without reviling is unspeakably glorious. Surely this is one of the reasons why Paul calls his message "the gospel of the glory of Christ" (2 Corinthians 4 v 4) and "the gospel of the glory of the blessed God" (1 Timothy 1 v 11).

So the double remedy for our inveterate craving for power and self-exaltation is first that this sin is covered by the blood of Christ, and second that God opens our eyes to see the glory of Christ as the satisfaction of our souls. Our power-craving souls are set free by seeing and savoring a superior glory to the glory of self-exaltation. God has reversed the exchange of Romans 1 v 23—the exchange of the glory of God for images, such as the image of myself, where I seek glory for myself by exalting myself above others in power. God has opened our eyes to the folly and ugliness and deadliness of vying with

---

6 For more on this "peculiar glory" of Christ, and how it relates to how we can know the Word of God (his Son and his Scriptures), see John Piper, *A Peculiar Glory: How the Christian Scriptures Reveal Their Complete Truthfulness* (Crossway, 2016), especially chapter 13.

him for power. He has opened our eyes to the beauty that all power really is his. He has granted us to see that the most glorious display of his power is in the power of the gospel, where Christ walked through weakness into everlasting dominion and glory.

5

DELIVERANCE: THE RETURN OF THE SUN TO THE CENTER

There is a remedy—a deliverance—that would not only rescue us from the dangers of money, sex, and power, but would unleash their potential as we used and enjoyed them in the ways that, and for the reasons why, God gave them to us in the first place.

That remedy is to wake up to the all-satisfying glory of God. If that could happen—if the blazing beauty of the sun could be restored to the center of the solar system of our lives—then money, sex, and power would gradually, or suddenly, come back into their God-glorifying orbits, and we would discover what we were made for. We would escape the broken solar system we made when we exchanged God for something else.

ALL CREATION EXISTS TO SAY, "GOD IS GOD; I AM NOT"

What we have seen is that power is a capacity to pursue what we value. Money is a cultural symbol that can be exchanged in pursuit of what we value. And sex is one of the pleasures that we do value. So the potential for good in money, sex, and power lies in the way they display the value of God. God is the supreme value in the universe. The universe was created to communicate that value for the enjoyment of God's people.

Therefore, money exists so that it will be plain by the way we use it that God is more to be desired than money. Sex exists so that it will be plain that God is more to be desired than sex. And power exists so that it will be plain that admiring and depending on his power is more to be desired than exalting our own. All things exist to serve the ultimate aim of God in creation—the display of the infinite beauty and worth of God, climaxing in the Christ-exalting reclamation of fallen mankind for the everlasting imaging and enjoyment of God's glory.

And underneath these realities are the foundational truths that we were created to glorify and thank God (Romans 1 v 21)—that is, to treasure the glory of God over all things, to be amazed at his glory, to admire his beauty, to enjoy him and all his perfections, to be satisfied in him, and to find a deep, settled contentment in his all-satisfying fellowship. In this way, our lives—in the path of truth and love and justice—begin to reflect the glory we admire and we glorify our all-satisfying God. That's what we were made for. That would be our highest pleasure, and his greatest glory.

DEADLY PLANETS WITHOUT A SUN

But since the fall, we have all "exchanged the glory of ... God" for other things (Romans 1 v 23), and we reflexively find those other things more interesting, more valuable, and more satisfying than God, which is a great insult to him (v 21). And if not remedied and atoned for, this ongoing insult will bring us to eternal and deserved ruin (2 v 8).

We have seen the seriousness of our situation in the analogy of the solar system. The preference for other things over God is like replacing the sun at the center of the solar system of our lives with an inferior planet—such as money, sex, power or simply self—so that the planets of money and sex and power, which were once held in their God-glorifying orbits, are flying wildly and dangerously out of orbit.

Money is zigzagging everywhere, awakening covetousness and greed, and becoming the currency of "pride in possessions"(1 John 2 v 16, see ESV footnote) and dishonesty and anxiety and theft and bribery and embezzling. Sex is spiking up and down erratically in fornication and adultery and pornography and public nudity—or even the fear of sexuality, as if it were not a good gift from God. In all these sins we turn God's glory into shame, and our shame into so-called human glory. And power is thrusting itself through everything in every manner of self-exalting control and domination and exploitation.

All of this ruin and destruction come because we have exchanged the glory of God—the blazing sun—for other things—things that cannot hold our lives together. We find more pleasure in these other things, and other persons, than we do in God. The psalmist tells us in Psalm 16 v 11, "In [his] presence there is fullness of joy; at [his] right hand are pleasures forevermore." But God says in Jeremiah 2 v 13, "My people have committed two evils: they have forsaken me, the fountain of living waters, and hewed out cisterns for themselves, broken cisterns that can hold no water." We were made to live with God as the all-satisfying center of our lives, with everything else in good, godly, happy orbit. Instead, we have a solar system with competing gravitational centers, and nothing else flying in its right orbit.

UNDESERVED DELIVERANCE

But there is deliverance. We have glimpsed this remedy in the previous chapters. Now we look at how God restores himself to the center of our lives so that we might enjoy him as our greatest satisfaction; in the next chapter, we will see how this rediscovery of God-centeredness puts the planets of money, sex, and power back into their God-glorifying orbits.

In spite of the way we have all insulted God by our preference for other things, God, in his unspeakable mercy, has done what we cannot do for ourselves, to give us a future and a hope in him. He did something on the cross. He did something when he gave us spiritual life and inclined our heart to believe in Jesus. And he does something every day. The result is that we find ourselves—unworthy though we be—in his presence and at his right hand, where there is fullness of joy and pleasures forevermore. And everything in our life changes.

JUSTIFICATION: DELIVERANCE FROM REAL, LEGAL GUILT

First, God did something on the cross to bring us into his presence with joy. "Christ also suffered once for sins, the righteous for the unrighteous, that he might bring us to God" (1 Peter 3 v 18).

If you have become fearful and discouraged by the dangers we have been talking about, because you have fallen far short of the glory of God (Romans 3 v 23), take heart. That is precisely why Jesus came into the world. That is why, as Peter says, the righteous died for the unrighteous. Remember Romans 1 v 18—it was in "unrighteousness" that we suppressed the truth of God's glory. That unrighteous, self-justifying, God-exchanging suppression of truth is what Christ died for. The righteous suffered for the unrighteous.

None of us have ever loved God as God deserves. Even as Christians, our faith and love are imperfect. Christ died for this—all of it. To what end? "That he might bring us to God" (1 Peter 3 v 18). The ultimate aim of the cross—the death of Jesus—is not the forgiveness of sins, nor the justification of the ungodly, nor the removal of God's wrath, nor deliverance from hell, as infinitely precious as those are. They are all means to the ultimate end. Peter tells us the ultimate end: He "suffered … that he might bring us to God." The presence of God. The sight of God. The knowledge of God. The enjoyment of God. Christ died to bring us here, though none of us do now, or ever will, deserve to be here.

In Christ's perfect life and death in our place, all

the legal barriers between us and God were removed. That is what justification means. Our punishment was endured by Christ. God's holy and just wrath was satisfied. The righteous demands of God's law were met in him:

> [9] Since, therefore, we have now been justified by his blood, much more shall we be saved by him from the wrath of God. [10] For if while we were enemies we were reconciled to God by the death of his Son, much more, now that we are reconciled, shall we be saved by his life. (Romans 5 v 9-10)

When we are united to Christ by faith, his righteousness is counted as ours, and God justly looks on us as innocent and righteous in Christ. So Paul could say that he would be "found in him, not having a right eousness of my own that comes from the law, but that which comes through faith in Christ, the righteousness from God that depends on faith" (Philippians 3 v 9). God accomplished this for all who are in Christ by making Christ to be sin for us, so that we might be righteous in him:

> For our sake he made him to be sin who knew no sin, so that in him we might become the righteousness of God. (2 Corinthians 5 v 21)

In this way, all legal barriers were removed between us and God. Now we may enjoy peace. "Since we have been justified by faith, we have peace with God through our Lord Jesus Christ" (Romans 5 v 1). And the ultimate value of this peace is that it enables us to be in the very presence of the all-glorious, all-satisfying God, where there is fullness of joy and pleasures forever (1 Peter 3 v 18; Psalm 16 v 11).

NEW BIRTH: DELIVERANCE FROM SPIRITUAL DEATH AND BLINDNESS

Just as God secured our justification through his Son at the cross, so he then applied that justification to us through his Spirit by opening our blind eyes to turn to him in faith. And as he gave us this sight, he caused us to see himself as the all-satisfying center of our affections.

Our problem is not only an external legal one, but an internal one. We are morally diseased. We are spiritually dead. The benefits of justification would never come to us if God did not work a miracle of change in us. We are in danger not only of the wrath of God because of our guilt; we are also in the bondage of our own deadness to God's glory. As fallen sinners, we do not see God as glorious, and we do not treasure God above all things. This is why money, sex, and power are so dangerous. They look more attractive than God, because we are spiritually blind to the all-satisfying beauty of God.

For this to change, there must be not only justification, but also regeneration—new birth. "Jesus answered Nicodemus, 'Truly, truly, I say to you, unless one is born again he cannot see the kingdom of God'" (John 3 v 3). Without this profound change in our nature—from spiritually dead to spiritually alive—we cannot see God for who he is. And we cannot trust him or treasure him as we ought. We are blind and need God to work the miracle of sight. This is sometimes referred to as God's effectual calling—it's the way Jesus called Lazarus, who had been dead for four days: "He cried out with a loud voice, 'Lazarus, come out.' The man who had died came out" (John 11 v 43-44). The call itself created what it commanded: life. And Lazarus, the dead man, lived and obeyed.

One of the most important texts on this miracle of God calling people out of darkness and death and blindness into light and life is 2 Corinthians 4 v 3-6:

> [3] Even if our gospel is veiled, it is veiled to those who are perishing. [4] In their case the god of this world has blinded the minds of the unbelievers, to keep them from seeing the light of the gospel of the glory of

> Christ, who is the image of God … [6] For God, who
> said, "Let light shine out of darkness," has shone in
> our hearts to give the light of the knowledge of the
> glory of God in the face of Jesus Christ.

All unbelievers, Paul says, are blind to the glory of
God in Christ. And Satan is hard at work confirming
and deepening that blindness by every means possible. This is a darkness that cannot see the all-satisfying glory of God in Christ; and so this is the darkness
that exchanges the glory of God for other things—the
darkness that deposes God from his place at the center
of the solar system of our lives, and puts ridiculous
and inadequate lesser planets in his place.

Look carefully at our condition in verse 4: "The god
of this world has blinded the minds of the unbelievers, to keep them from seeing the light of the gospel
of the glory of Christ, who is the image of God."
What can't we see? We can't see the supreme brightness—the light of the glory of Christ in the gospel.
People can hear the gospel—the greatest work of God
in the history of the universe—and not be moved, just
as people can stand before the Alps or the Himalayas
or the galaxies and shrug their shoulders and turn on
the television. That is our condition.

But because Christ died for us, God is able, with

perfect justice, to do verse 6 for us. Listen, and ask if he has done it for you. "God, who said, 'Let light shine out of darkness,' has shone in our hearts to give the light of the knowledge of the glory of God in the face of Jesus Christ." In the same way that God created light at the beginning of creation with a sovereign call—"Let there be light!"—so God does that same thing in the human heart. This is called new birth, or regeneration, or effectual calling. God speaks and, by his all-powerful word, causes us to see the light of the glory of God in the face of Christ. As Peter says, he "called you out of darkness into his marvelous light" (1 Peter 2 v 9). The call creates the sight of the light of the glory of God. The evil exchange of Romans 1 v 23 (the glory of God for images) is over! The idolatry is over. The great insult is over. We see with clarity and we savor the glory of God in Christ.

Now there is one more thing that God does to secure our deliverance from the dangers of money, sex, and power.

DELIVERANCE INTO THE LIKENESS OF HIS GLORY
God does not stop revealing to us the glory of Christ in his word. He starts at new birth, and he keeps on revealing the glory of Christ. Our new life started with

a miracle—and it continues with a miracle. The ongoing miracle that God works by his Spirit is that we become increasingly like the one we admire and enjoy—him.

Just a few verses before the text we already looked at in 2 Corinthians 4, Paul writes:

> We all, with unveiled face, beholding the glory of the Lord, are being transformed into the same image from one degree of glory to another. (3 v 18)

The words "beholding" and "being transformed" are present tense, which means ongoing action—not once for all, but continual. "*Beholding* the glory of the Lord, we *are being* transformed." This is what God does daily as we look to him in his word. It is what he does weekly in the preaching of his word in gathered worship. And it is what, I pray, he is doing right now as you read.

Many Christians, especially newer Christians, long for a method of discipleship that will change them quickly by just following a few clear and doable steps. I would caution you from pressing too hard for such a foolproof method. Such approaches to growth and change often lead to disillusionment, and sometimes to a crisis of faith—why is this not working for me?

God's way toward growth is more like the watering of a plant, or feeding a baby, than the building of a wall brick by brick with a manual in our hand. When you build a wall that way, you can see every brick put in place, and measure the progress. We hold the brick; we apply the mortar to hold it in place; we place the brick. *Voila!* Growth! Christian growth is not like that. It's more organic, less in our control, and usually slower.

Beware of schemes that put things in your control, and promise more than they can deliver. Consider this picture from 1 Peter 2 v 2-3:

> [2] Like newborn infants, long for the pure spiritual milk, that by it you may grow up into salvation—[3] if indeed you have tasted that the Lord is good.

The picture is of a child growing. At the end of the day, can you see the growth? No. At end of a week? Not really. But after a year—yes! Did you control the growth by adding inches and pounds? No. You fed the child. You cleaned the child. You protected the child from harm. And God gave the growth.

Peter tells us to "long for the pure spiritual milk" in the way a baby desires food when he or she is hungry. In other words, really desire it! Cry out for it. Don't be quiet till you have it. What is the milk? Two clues.

First, Peter had just described the new birth of a baby Christian in 1 v 22 25. He said that "you have been born again ... through the living and abiding word of God ... And this word is the good news that was preached to you." So the life-giving means that God used to create a new creature in Christ—the way he caused the new birth—is by means of the word of God, especially the sweetness of the gospel. So when he says, two verses later, that this Christian should desire the spiritual milk for growth, it is natural to think he is still referring to the word that gave them life in the first place.

The second clue that Peter is thinking about the word when he refers to the milk is in the next verse (2 v 3): "if indeed you have tasted that the Lord is good." The word "tasted" signals to us that Peter is still thinking about desiring drink. And here the taste of the drink is "that the Lord is good." So I conclude that the milk that we are to desire for growth is the goodness and kindness of the Lord revealed in his word. Or to put it another way, reading the word with a specific intention to taste the goodness of the Lord as we read.

Peter says the effect of this regular feeding on the spiritual milk of God's goodness in his word will be to "grow up into salvation." Our growth will be toward the climax of our total transformation when Christ returns. And in the meantime there will be real, but incremental, and sometimes slow, growth.

This growth is a miracle and not entirely manageable by us. To be sure, we are not to be passive. But the decisive spiritual work belongs to God. Jesus told a parable to emphasize this divine work in growth:

> [26] The kingdom of God is as if a man should scatter seed on the ground. [27] He sleeps and rises night and day, and the seed sprouts and grows; he knows not how. [28] The earth produces by itself, first the blade, then the ear, then the full grain in the ear. [29] But when the grain is ripe, at once he puts in the sickle, because the harvest has come. (Mark 4 v 26-29)

This parable is about the kingdom of God in the world. But the principle applies to the kingdom of God bringing about growth in the believer. The point of the parable is that, even though we sow seed (as we drink the spiritual milk of God's kindness in his word), nevertheless, the blade and ear and grain come into being "he knows not how." It is not in our control. God gives the growth. Or as Paul said, about the growth of faith among the Corinthians:

> [6] I planted, Apollos watered, but God gave the growth. [7] So neither he who plants nor he who waters is anything, but only God who gives the growth.
>
> (1 Corinthians 3 v 6-7)

Now back to the point of this section: God transforms us and brings the planets of our lives into Christ-exalting, soul-satisfying orbit by opening our eyes to see his glory in the word. "Beholding the glory of the Lord, [we] are being transformed into the same image from one degree of glory to another" (2 Corinthians 3 v 18). In other words, what happens when we regularly drink the word, and taste the kindness of the Lord in the word, is that God opens our eyes to see the wonders of his glory. His kindness—his grace in action—is the apex of his glory. God grants us to see "wondrous things" from his word (Psalm 119 v 18). He grants us the experience of Samuel at Shiloh: "The LORD revealed himself to Samuel at Shiloh by the word of the LORD" (1 Samuel 3 v 21). And seeing the Lord himself, in the limitless dimensions of his greatness and beauty, we are shaped by what we see. He conforms us to himself. We become most like what we admire most.

BEHOLDING THE LORD'S GLORY WITH MONEY, SEX, AND POWER

For example, when I drink in the word about Jesus being so unencumbered by possessions that he had no place to lay his head, my amazement at his poverty (a poverty that made many rich) moves me, shapes me and frees me from my love affair with money.

> Someone said to [Jesus], "I will follow you wherever you go." And Jesus said to him, "Foxes have holes, and birds of the air have nests, but the Son of Man has nowhere to lay his head." (Luke 9 v 57-58)

When I read that story, I meet Jesus. I see the glory of Jesus, who "though he was rich, yet for your sake he became poor, so that you by his poverty might become rich" (2 Corinthians 8 v 9). I see him. I love him. I am drawn to him. And I find him giving himself to me. His freedom from money starts to give me freedom from money. He is more admirable than all the wealthy tycoons on Wall Street. The desire to be with him and like him is rising like a passion in my heart. This is what happens when we see his glory in the word.

Or when I look at his sexual life, the same thing happens. Decades of virility—yet not one sinful moment of yielding to a lustful thought or an immoral act. Women were hanging on his words and following him around. Former prostitutes wept over him and wiped his bare feet with their hair. He spoke one on one with a woman who had had five husbands and was living with a sixth lover who was not her husband.

He lived a life that from one angle could be viewed as charged with sexual temptation. But he never sinned. He denied himself perfectly without denying the goodness of sexuality. He was the most fully human being who ever existed, and never had sexual intercourse. As I watch him, I love him. I admire him. I stand in awe of his purity of mind and body. And I find myself growing in hatred of my own little compromises. I find myself longing to be pure and to be found holy at the last day, and to be above reproach. His glorious purity is contagious.

Or when I look into the word and behold the glory of how Jesus used his power, I am awed. In the Garden of Gethsemane, when he was about to be arrested, he said to his angry disciples, "Do you think that I cannot appeal to my Father, and he will at once send me more than twelve legions of angels?" (Matthew 26 v 53). Yes, he could. And he didn't. He had great power at his disposal, and he did not use it. He walked willingly and sovereignly to his death: "No one takes [my life] from me, but I lay it down of my own accord" (John 10 v 18).

Jesus's power was on display mightily in the hour of his greatest weakness. For example, the night before his death, he said to Simon Peter, "Simon, Simon, behold, Satan demanded to have you, that he might sift you like wheat, but I have prayed for you that your faith may not fail. And when you have turned again, strengthen your brothers" (Luke 22 v 31-32). Notice the word "when," not "if": "When you have turned." Jesus was in charge that night. Every detail of his mock trial and execution was going the way he and the Father had planned it. Satan was at work—but every move the evil one made was tying the noose tighter around his own neck.

What do you feel when you watch the glories of Jesus shine through in this way? I feel wonder. Admiration. Trembling love. Head-shaking fear that if I had been there, I would have let him down. Desire— O how I desire to walk with him and know him and be like him. And in these moments of admiration, I find myself being changed.

This is what I mean when I say that God's miracle of new birth does not stop with our conversion. He goes on changing us. And he does it by opening our eyes to the glory of Jesus in the word. "Beholding the glory of the Lord, [we] are being transformed." The way we use our money, the way we express our sexuality, and the way we exert our power, are transformed. What that transformation looks like is what we turn to in the final chapter.

DEPLOYMENT: THE NEW ORBITS FOR MONEY, SEX, AND POWER

When we are born again, and God grants us the ability to recover the glory of God as our greatest treasure, and our sweetest pleasure, the sun returns to its place at the center of the solar system of our lives, and all the planets start to return to their God-glorifying orbits.

So let's look at some examples of what happens to money, sex, and power when we live as those whose our sins are forgiven and who live in the light; when we are born again, and the glory of God in Christ has been restored as the greatest treasure and sweetest pleasure of our lives.

DEPLOYING MONEY FOR THE GLORY OF GOD

We turn first to 2 Corinthians 8. Paul is writing to the Corinthians to motivate them to be generous in their contribution of money for the poor saints in Jerusalem. He is taking a collection among the churches for the poor, and he wants them to be ready when he comes. So he lifts up the example of the believers in Macedonia:

> [1] We want you to know, brothers, about the grace of God that has been given among the churches of Macedonia, [2] for in a severe test of affliction, their abundance of joy and their extreme poverty have overflowed in a wealth of generosity on their part.
>
> (v 1-2)

God's grace in the gospel had come to Macedonia, and people had been dramatically converted. The fruit of that conversion was seen most astonishingly in their joy, and then in what their joy produced: "In a severe test of affliction, their abundance of joy and their extreme poverty" (v 2). Notice they experienced joy and affliction. So their abundant joy was not in the absence of affliction—evidently affliction had increased since they became Christians. And notice they knew joy and poverty—"extreme poverty"! So their joy was not owing to the absence of poverty, or to the absence of affliction. This was a joy in the midst of affliction and poverty. What, then, was their joy in?

It was in the grace of God. The grace of God had been given (v 1): that is, Christ had been preached, who "suffered ... the righteous for the unrighteous, that he might bring us to God" (1 Peter 3 v 18). God's grace had opened their eyes to God's glory. They knew God. God was no longer their enemy; they were reconciled. They were rejoicing in the hope of the glory of God and eternal life with him (Romans 5 v 2). And this joy was so strong that it was not overcome by affliction or poverty.

What was the effect? "In a severe test of affliction, their abundance of joy and their extreme poverty have overflowed in a wealth of generosity on their part" (2 Corinthians 8 v 2). Their joy overflowed in generous giving of money in the midst of poverty. This is a picture of what happens to our money when our joy is no longer in that money but rather is in God. We are freed from the greed and fear of covetousness, and our money becomes the instrument of love.

Our money becomes the visible extension of our joy in God, directed toward others. That's what the text says. It is our joy that overflows. It is the joy in God that is flowing in the generosity to others. The point is not that we take our money and burden someone else with this dangerous material! The point is to reveal, by our love, that God is so satisfying that we can find our joy in giving rather than getting—that "it is more blessed to give than to receive" (Acts 20 v 35). Our hope is that the beneficiaries of our overflowing joy will see the real gift: namely, a picture of the all-satisfying glory of God's grace.

This is what you find again and again in the New Testament, especially the book of Hebrews:

- "You had compassion on those in prison, and you joyfully accepted the plundering of your property, since you knew that you yourselves had a better possession and an abiding one." (10 v 34)
- "[Moses chose] to be mistreated with the people of God ... [because] he considered the reproach of Christ greater wealth than the treasures of Egypt, for he was looking to the reward." (11 v 25-26)
- "Keep your life free from love of money, and be content with what you have, for he has said, 'I will never leave you nor forsake you.'" (13 v 5-6)

Treasuring God above all things turns money into the currency of worship and love. The planet of money comes into its God-appointed orbit, and as it moves with its face to the blazing sun, it shines brighter and brighter with the beauty of God in acts of generosity.[7]

GOD-CENTERED JOY IN THE MARKETPLACE

Of course, the role of money in life and society is vastly larger than special gifts to the poor. And the teaching here has implications for every use of money in the Christian life—from allowances for children, to investment in the stock market, to gathering capital for a business startup. When I sum up Paul's point in 2 Corinthians 8 v 2 by saying, "Our money becomes the visible extension of our joy in God, directed toward others," I don't mean that this is relevant only for mercy ministry and charity. I mean that this truth is our essential guide to payrolls, investments, economic policy, global trade and a hundred other ways in which we must handle money.

Until a Christian businessman has experienced the grace of God in the forgiveness of sins, and the

---

7 These acts of generosity are not only the kind that happen daily in the way we treat people in "[giving] to the one who asks" (Matthew 5 v 42, NIV), but also in the more thoughtful, strategic efforts on a community and global scale, as represented in Steve Corbett and Brian Fikkert, *When Helping Hurts: How to Alleviate Poverty Without Hurting the Poor … and Yourself* (Moody, 2014); and Wayne Grudem and Barry Asmus, *Poverty of Nations: A Sustainable Solution* (Crossway, 2013).

renovation of his desires in the new birth, and the progressive transformation that comes from steadily looking to Jesus, he will not handle his money in the marketplace in a way that shows that his joy is in supremely in Jesus. I don't mean that this experience is all we need. The complexities of business and economics are enormous. Many biblical principles and much wisdom from real life are needed to display the glories of Christ in the marketplace of the world. But I do mean that the supremacy of the all-satisfying Christ at the center of life is essential for Christ-exalting business, as well as Christ-exalting giving.

In fact, a whole book could be written on the relationship between God-centered mercy to the poor and the pursuit of profitable market strategies. They are not unrelated. The vast poverty of the world will never be overcome merely by charitable generosity. The love awakened by the supremacy of the all-glorious God of grace not only pours itself out through sacrificial charitable generosity; it also presses itself into economic plans, and business practices, and governmental policies. I do not know enough to write about this in any detail. But I would point you to Wayne Grudem and Barry Asmus' book, *The Poverty of Nations: A Sustainable Solution* (Crossway, 2013), as an example of what I mean.

What we need to note *here* is that the Christ-exalting potential of money resides not only in the way we give gifts, but also in the way we spend and save our money and do our business. The decisive truth that I am focusing on is the same in all these cases. Does the all-satisfying beauty of Christ have the gravitational weight at the center of your life to control not only the orbit of giving, but also the orbits of spending, and selling, and trading, and investing, and setting salaries, and paying taxes, and creating businesses, and shaping trade laws and governmental policies? The potentials of money for doing good and glorifying God are just as real in these economic spheres as they are in our personal relations with the needy in our neighborhood. The central issue is always: Is God our supreme treasure? And do we want that for others? Is our use of money an overflow of our grasp of and wonder at the grace and glory of God?

SAVORING SEX FOR THE GLORY OF GOD
In 1 Timothy 4 v 1-5, Paul confronts certain ascetic, pleasure-renouncing false teachers who believed that sex in marriage and eating foods freely were not the

way that Christians should use their bodies. And Paul called these false teachings demonic.

> [1] Now the Spirit expressly says that in later times some will depart from the faith by devoting themselves to deceitful spirits and teachings of demons, [2] through the insincerity of liars whose consciences are seared, [3] who forbid marriage and require abstinence from foods… (v 1-3)

That's the false teaching. Now here's Paul's response, starting in the middle of verse 3:

> [3] that [that is, the marriage and the food] God created to be received with thanksgiving by those who believe and know the truth. [4] For everything created by God is good, and nothing is to be rejected if it is received with thanksgiving, [5] for it is made holy by the word of God and prayer. (v 3-5)

For those who know the truth of the gospel, and who revel in the word of God concerning the all-satisfying glory of God, and who pray (Hallowed be your name!), and who dedicate everything to God, the sex of marriage and the pleasures of food are made holy—that is, sex and food are set apart from the sinful use of the world, and made pure and precious and beautiful by participation in the goodness of God.

We are not supposed to be embarrassed by the forthright sensuality of sexual love in marriage as the Bible portrays it—sometimes graphically:

> [18] Let your fountain be blessed, and rejoice in the wife of your youth, [19] a lovely deer, a graceful doe. Let her breasts fill you at all times with delight; be intoxicated always in her love. [20] Why should you be intoxicated, my son, with a forbidden woman and embrace the bosom of an adulteress? [21] For a man's ways are before the eyes of the LORD, and he ponders all his paths. (Proverbs 5 v 18-21)

It is no shame that "a man's ways are before ... the LORD" as his wife's breasts fill him at all times with delight. This is why God made her that way—and made him with those desires. In fact, that this delight in her is "before" the Lord points to the truth that all our joy in what God has made is meant to be a delight in God. There is something of his glory in all the glories of the world. We are not meant to revel in his creation instead of him or more than him but because of him, and because there is something of him in all that is good and beautiful. The heavens are telling the glory of God. We are to see it. And worship him. So it is with the breasts of our wives. Those breasts are telling us about the glory of God, the goodness of God, the beauty of God, and more. We are to see it and worship him as we enjoy them.

The Song of Solomon is in the Bible, among other reasons, to make sure that we take seriously the exquisite physical pleasures between a bride and a groom as a picture of Christ and his church. The point is not that we nullify the physical pleasures of this Song by seeing only a portrayal of Christ and the church. To be sure, we are to see Christ and the church in the relationship of the Song of Solomon in the way Paul sees it in Ephesians 5 v 22-33. But the danger is that we *only* see the metaphorical dimension, not the physical one. Instead, we should let the Song stun us, that the kind of relationship God designed between man and woman as the image of the covenant-keeping pleasures between Christ and his church can be described with words like these from husband to bride:

> [5] Your two breasts are like two fawns, twins of a gazelle, that graze among the lilies. [6] Until the day breathes and the shadows flee, I will go away to the mountain of myrrh and the hill of frankincense. [7] You are altogether beautiful, my love; there is no flaw in you. (Song of Solomon 4 v 5-7)

³ Your two breasts are like two fawns, twins of a ga-
zelle. ⁴ Your neck is like an ivory tower. Your eyes are
pools in Heshbon, by the gate of Bath-rabbim. Your
nose is like a tower of Lebanon, which looks toward
Damascus. ⁵ Your head crowns you like Carmel, and
your flowing locks are like purple; a king is held captive in the tresses. ⁶ How beautiful and pleasant you
are, O loved one, with all your delights! ⁷ Your stature
is like a palm tree, and your breasts are like its clusters. ⁸ I say I will climb the palm tree and lay hold of
its fruit. Oh may your breasts be like clusters of the
vine, and the scent of your breath like apples, ⁹ and
your mouth like the best wine.

(Song of Solomon 7 v 3-9)

And like this, with words from the bride:

³ I had put off my garment; how could I put it on?
I had bathed my feet; how could I soil them? ⁴ My
beloved put his hand to the latch, and my heart was
thrilled within me. ⁵ I arose to open to my beloved,
and my hands dripped with myrrh, my fingers with
liquid myrrh, on the handles of the bolt.

(Song of Solomon 5 v 3-5)

HANNAH'S QUESTION

While this book was with the publisher, I did another *Ask Pastor John* podcast, and a woman called Hannah asked:

> How is sex between a husband and wife a practical example of Christ and his church?

Here is part of how I replied:[8]

> I will mention three things. And I don't doubt that these are the lowlands of the Himalayas of glory that better people than I could climb into and explain.
>
> First, very prominent in Ephesians 5 is the asymmetry, lack of symmetry, between the roles of husband and wife. She is to submit to his Christ-like, loving, sacrificial headship. But there is, just as clearly, a mutuality and reciprocity in seeking to bless and satisfy the other as leadership and submission find their way toward maximum mutual pleasure. In 1 Corinthians 7 v 4 Christ says that the man does not have authority over his body, but the woman does, and the woman does not have authority over her body, but the man does, which creates, if you are a logic-chopper, a total stalemate.

---

8 Audio available at desiringgod.org/interviews/by-series/ask-pastor-john

But Paul clearly doesn't mean for there to be a stalemate in the marriage bed. The point is that the wife often has desires and the husband in love should want to satisfy them and work to do so; and the husband often has desires and the wife in love should want to satisfy them and give a similar effort.

But as they proceed, the way the man pursues the satisfying of his wife is in the capacity of a head and the initiative taker. And this doesn't rule out her own particular kinds of initiatives, but it does set the tone and establish a context in which he is felt to be the strong, caring, loving, creative leader in this event which is what Christ and the church are about.

And so my first answer is that in the act of sexual relations in marriage, the beauty and the complexity and the mystery of headship and submission in their most satisfying expressions are being realized.

Second, the reason the rare and extraordinary pleasure of simultaneous orgasm is as great as it is, is not only to point us to the ecstasies of knowing Christ, but also to give us a very taste of those ecstasies. In other words, when Jesus says that he is the bread of life (John 6 v 35, 48), he means for us to taste something of his life in our favorite bread from some good German bakery.

The pleasure of the emblem when it is consecrated to God becomes a foretaste and a pleasure of the thing itself: Christ in the bread.

So it is with the pleasures of the marriage bed as an emblem of Christ and the church in fellowship. When a married couple loves each other and brings that love to climax in sexual consummation and lies there still, restful, thankful at the end, their hearts should be brimming with how wonderful Jesus Christ is: that he would give them such pleasures and that he would show them in those pleasures what he is like and how precious is the church's relationship to her husband.

Third, I would say that metaphors in general are lesser realities than what they are metaphors of. So a wedding ring is precious. I still have mine on. I think I have only taken mine off my finger twice in 46 years of marriage. So my wedding ring is precious to me. But a wedding ring is not as precious as the marriage and the pleasures of the marriage that it signifies. And sexual pleasure in marriage is precious, but not as precious as what it signifies in relation to Jesus.

Jesus said that in the age to come there will be no marriage or giving in marriage (Luke 20 v 35). Now that may seem like a colossal disappointment for those of us who have enjoyed the pleasures of the marriage bed. But what if someone said, *In the future I am going to take away your wedding ring, and all you are going to have is heightened ecstasies that it stood for.* Would you be disappointed? Well, a little bit, but not very long. No, you wouldn't. In other words, the sexual pleasures in marriage point not only to the present pleasures of knowing and loving Christ, but they also point to the age to come, where the ring—that is, the pleasures in this analogy—will be taken away, and we will experience the reality in such greater measure of pleasure that we will wonder how we could have ever been satisfied with the best sex in the world.

THE WORLD HAS STOLEN WHAT BELONGS TO BELIEVERS

All this is part of what Paul had in mind in 1 Timothy 4 v 3-5 when he said:

> [3] God created [it] to be received with thanksgiving by those who believe and know the truth … [5] It is made holy by the word of God and prayer.

Sex is for "those who believe and know the truth." We might lose sight of this, since Hollywood has ripped the curtains of the sacred marriage bed and turned a luxuriant, holy pleasure into a cheap spectator sport. We might be tempted to think that sex is so sinfully misused, and is so universally undermining to the all-satisfying beauty of Christ's holiness that maybe we Christians should have nothing to do with it, except for the purposes of having children.

Paul says the opposite. The world has stolen what belongs to believers, and believers should take it back. Sex belongs to Christians, because sex belongs to God. "God created [it] to be received with thanksgiving by those who believe and know the truth." If it is used by those who do not believe and know the truth, it is prostituted. They have exchanged the glory of God for images. They have torn sex from its God-appointed place within God-given marriage. But they do not know what they are doing, and the price they will pay in this life and the next is incalculable.

The pleasures of sex are meant for believers. They are designed for their greatest expression by the children of God. He saves his richest gifts for his children. And as we enjoy his gift of sex, we say, by our covenant faithfulness to our spouse, that God is greater than sex. And the pleasures of sex are themselves an overflow of God's own goodness. This pleasure is less than what we will know fully in him at his right hand; but it is more than the world will ever experience in its misuse of sex. And in that pleasure, we taste something of his very exquisiteness.

In chapter one, I defined sex as "experiencing erotic stimulation, or seeking to get the experience, or seeking to give the experience." I have not separated these three parts in this last chapter. The focus has been on how we experience the sexual pleasures of the body and mind. But I hope it is plain that there are implications for how we seek this, and how we give it. I believe that if we know the key to glorifying God in the very taste of sexual pleasure, the implications for seeking it and giving it will be obvious. When the preciousness and pleasures of Christ are supreme, all dimensions of sex, including experiencing pleasure, seeking pleasure, giving pleasure—and abstinence from pleasure!—will all find their biblical and Christ-exalting expression.

Everything God made is good. Everything is for the sake of worship toward God and love toward people. And this is true both in the feasting and the fasting, in the sexual union and in abstinence. Sex is made for the glory of Christ—for the Christ-exalting glory of covenant-keeping faithfulness in marriage, and for the glory of Christ-exalting chastity in singleness.[9] It is always good. Sex is always an occasion to show that the Giver of sex is better than sex. When the all-satisfying glory of God returns as the blazing center of the solar system of our lives, the planet of sex—shall we call her Venus?—moves into her God-appointed, Christ-exalting, glorious orbit.

LIVING IN POWER FOR THE GLORY OF GOD

Finally, when the glory of God's all-prevailing, all-sustaining, all-supplying power is our joy, rather than the exaltation of our own power, we are freed to live powerfully in the power of God. When we grasp for power as a way of exalting ourselves and lording it over others, we surrender our God-given power to exalt him. But when we turn from self-exaltation in pride to God-exaltation in humility, we gain God's power to serve others, not to lord anything over anybody. This happy lowliness and sacrificial servanthood displays the all-sufficiency and glory of God's power to meet every need (Philippians 4 v 19; 2 Corinthians 9 v 8).

We are content to be jars of clay because this shows

9 In *This Momentary Marriage: A Parable of Permanence* (Crossway, 2012), I wrote two chapters on singleness in which I tried to work out the implications of how the sexuality of a non-married follower of Christ is meant to work out for the glory of God.

the power of God, which is the aim of creation and the aim of our new life in Christ. "We have this treasure in jars of clay, to show that the surpassing power belongs to God and not to us" (2 Corinthians 4 v 7). This is our joy.

We are content in our weaknesses because Christ has promised to step in and be the strength that we need, which in turn displays his glory, not ours. Jesus told Paul (as he tells us), "My grace is sufficient for you, for my power is made perfect in weakness." "Therefore," Paul responds, "I will boast all the more gladly of my weaknesses" (2 Corinthians 12 v 9). This is what it means to have the planet of power come back into orbit with the glory of God's power at the center of our solar system. We love to be the place where Christ's power, not ours, is exalted.

A PRECIOUS AND FAVORITE VERSE

How many hundreds of times in my life have I leaned on 1 Peter 4 v 11?

> Whoever serves, [let him do it] as one who serves by the strength that God supplies [Why?]—in order that in everything God may be glorified through Jesus Christ. To him belong glory and dominion forever and ever. Amen.

This is one of the clearest passages in the Bible for how power is meant to serve the purposes of God in the creation and redemption of the world. Servanthood and power are combined. Our service in his power.

It is a great mystery. Do you know what this feels like? We actually use our own thinking and our wills and our effort and our skills to help others; and yet, all the while we are not thinking and not willing and not exerting in our own strength, but in God's. What a miracle! This is the great work of the Holy Spirit as we look away from our selves in the act of service and trust the promise of God: "I will strengthen you, I will help you, I will uphold you with my righteous right hand" (Isaiah 41 v 10). Faith in God's promise is the channel through which the promised power comes.

And the Giver of the power gets the glory. That is the great goal. It is the best of arrangements: We get the help. He gets the glory. And as newborn, humble children of God, we are happy to have it so. Whatever makes our Father look great is what makes us happy. And when his glory makes us happy, he is glorified in our lives. This is why power exists—both his, and ours as his gift.

When God grants us power—and he does in many ways—his aim is that he will be glorified by the way that power is used. For example, Paul says in 1 Corinthians 2 v 4-5, "My speech and my message were not in plausible words of wisdom, but in demonstration of the Spirit and of power, so that your faith might not rest in the wisdom of men but in the power of God." Paul was granted to wield the power of the Spirit in his ministry—as all of us are called to do—but God's aim, and his, was not that the people would make much of him, but rather that they would see God and savor God and trust God as the all-powerful, all-wise, all-satisfying One.

As children of God who are justified by the blood of Christ and born again by his Spirit, and progressively transformed by beholding his glory in his word (as we saw in chapter 5), we never cease to need divine help to see the power of God as glorious. We are always at risk of craving the self-exaltation of power because we lose sight of the greatness and beauty of God's power on our behalf.

This is why Paul prays for the believers in Ephesus like this: that "the eyes of your hearts would be enlightened, that you may know … what is the immeasurable greatness of his power toward us who believe, according to the working of his great might" (Ephesians 1 v 18-19). The eyes of our heart are prone to become dim. We start to lose sight of the "immeasurable greatness of his power toward us"—and when that sight becomes dim, the inevitable craving that rises in its place is for our own power and our self-exaltation.

Therefore, we see that one of the ways that God delivers us from the danger of self-promoting use of power is through prayer. Paul prays for saints—Christians—that we would "know ... the immeasurable greatness of his power toward us who believe." If Paul prayed this, we should pray it for ourselves and for others. Beholding the glory of God's power, we will be changed; and being changed, we will not crave power to exalt ourselves. Prayer is both a reminder to ourselves and a plea to God that we would never forget who it is who has power—namely, God—and who it is who gives power—God—and who it is who deserves to be exalted by the way we use that power—God. Such a relentless focus on the centrality of God frees us from craving power for our own ends. When we are free from that craving, we will live for others and God will be glorified.

Perhaps we should look at one other illustration of the way Paul prays for God's power to be manifest in all our acts of obedience. Everything we do (as 1 Peter 4 v 11 implied) should be done in reliance on

God's power so that God gets the glory. Paul prays for this again and again. For example, in his second letter to the Thessalonians he writes, "To this end we always pray for you, that our God may make you worthy of his calling and may fulfill every resolve for good and every work of faith by his power (2 Thessalonians 1 v 11). Every resolve leading to every good deed should be done as a "work of faith"—that is, a work relying on God's grace. In that way, Paul says, it will be done "by his power." Paul prays this should be the aim and the fuel of all our deeds, and we should too. Pray that you would do works of faith in God's power, not yours.

WORTHY OF POWER

At the end of the age, when all of this history is over, and God has completed all his works, his people will worship him forever. And one of the acclamations we will make before him, over and over, is, "Worthy are you, our Lord and God, to receive … *power*, for you created all things, and by your will they existed and were created" (Revelation 4 v 11). We will sing, "Worthy is the Lamb who was slain, *to receive power*!" (5 v 12) and, "Blessing and … *power* and might be to our God forever and ever! Amen." (7 v 12) and, "Hallelujah!

Salvation and glory and *power* belong to our God" (19 v 1—all italics are mine).

In all the works of creation and redemption, God has had this great goal: "that I might show my power" (Romans 9 v 17); that all the world may "know that I am the LORD" (Exodus 14 v 4). This is his goal, not because his power is, alone, his essence, but because it is essential to the totality of his glory, which he aims to communicate in all his works. This is why he created the world and all of us: "everyone who is called by my name, whom I created for my glory" (Isaiah 43 v 7).

By means of justification, regeneration, and progressive transformation into God's likeness, God has reversed the great exchange (Romans 1 v 23) that ruined life and made us lovers of power rather than lovers of God. The possibility now exists—indeed, it is a reality for millions—to live in the power that God supplies, so that in everything God is glorified through Jesus Christ. It is a great redemption.

When we live like this, the planet of power is drawn into its humble, happy, fruitful, God-glorifying orbit by the sun of God's glory blazing at the center of all things.

Living in the light, therefore, is not simply basking in the sunshine of God's presence; it is being controlled by the massive gravitational effect of his all-satisfying beauty on all the parts—the planets—of our lives, including power, and sex, and money.

CONCLUSION

Money, sex, and power. Three precious gifts of God. Three dangers ready to destroy our pleasure, our wealth, our souls. Three beautiful possibilities for worship and love. The difference? Living in the light—"the light of the knowledge of the glory of God in the face of Jesus Christ"—satisfying the soul, setting us free, celebrating God, sending us to serve.

This is the blazing sun at the center of all things, and the reality that keeps all the planets flying joyfully in their place. Or we could say with the prophet Malachi, "The sun of righteousness shall rise with healing in its wings" (Malachi 4 v 2). We know that he meant Jesus Christ. The Son is the sun. John the Baptist's father, Zechariah, said as much when he described the arrival of the Messiah as "the sunrise [that] shall visit us from on high" (Luke 1 v 78). And what was the prophesied effect of the Son taking his place at the center of all things? "You shall go out leaping like calves from the stall" (Malachi 4 v 2).

WHERE WE HAVE BEEN

We began in chapter one with a picture of money, sex, and power as great icebergs floating in the sea of life. These are massive beneath the surface, with jagged edges that can rip a hole in your boat so deep it will sink to the bottom of the ocean. Chapters two to four described those dangers.

We also said in chapter one that there is another way to look at money, sex, and power. They may be floating islands of food, when the stores of our ship have run out, or fuel when we are stalled in the water, or the rarest fruit to sweeten our dreary sailing diet. That is what we have tried to describe in chapter six.

This was not my idea—to warn and to entice. This is the way the Bible is written. God knows what we need; so he put it in his word. We need clear, strong descriptions of the dangers of money, sex, and power, and of how vulnerable we are to making them our gods, the center and pull of our lives. And we need clear, strong descriptions of what glorious things they may become, when God alone is our God. So in this book, we have been battling on two fronts, just as we must throughout

MONEY, SEX & POWER

our lives. On the one hand, the planets of money, sex, and power threaten to usurp the place of the sun in the center of our lives. On the other hand, false religion threatens to drive them from the solar system as alien rocks that should have no place at all in our existence. The Bible shows us another way. When the Son takes his glorious place at the center of the solar system of our lives, the massive pull of his all-satisfying beauty corrects the erratic path of every planet, and makes the whole system sing with joy.

THE WIDE ANGLE LENS

But the Bible is not a self-help book on maximizing our potential through money, sex, and power. It is a book about the fall of man into hopeless blindness and folly—a book about how we have corrupted everything we have touched. And it is a book about God's intervention to save us from the destructive uses of money, sex, and power. So I have tried to weave that redemption—that remedy and deliverance—through the book, focusing on it in chapter five.

At the level of our own experience in life, the essence of the matter is that once we had exchanged the glory of God for other things. We preferred the gods of money, sex, and power to God himself. He was not our treasure; they were. If you are not yet trusting Christ as your treasure, they still are. So God addressed the essence of the matter through the death and resurrection of Christ, justifying us, regenerating us, and transforming our hearts, so that the devastating exchange has been reversed. God is being restored to the supreme place of value and beauty and pleasure in our lives.

As the sun rises to this glorious brightness in our souls, we are changed. Money, sex, and power no longer hold sway over us by their attraction. We are held by the attraction of God. This means that those gifts have now become pointers to what we value supremely: God himself. They are not nothing. But neither are they everything. They are God's gifts for our good and the good of the world. It is part of God's grace that his gifts for our good are also for his glory. When we learn to enjoy him in and above them all, these gifts will find their fullest goodness, and shine for his greatest glory.

THE NARROW LENS

As one who has devoted most of my life to thinking and preaching and writing about the teachings of the Bible, I am keenly aware of how easy it is for me to read without realizing—to see without seeing, hear without hearing, take in without living out. You may be like me in this way. If so, let me close by simply inviting you to pause and ask very seriously where in your life the centrality of God is not holding sway. What planets, in your daily experience, have flown off their God-ordained orbit? What evidence is there that the great gravitational pull at the center of your life is the glory of God? Are there ways in which money, or sex, or power have moved to the center of your solar system, or in which these gifts have been rejected altogether?

Can you joyfully say, "I am justified before God in Jesus Christ because I trust in him—my sins are forgiven"? Can you say, "I am born again—I am a new creation in Christ"? Can you joyfully say, "My blindness to the beauty of Jesus has been taken away. My eyes have been opened. I see the light of the gospel of the glory of Christ. He has become my supreme Treasure."

Do you make a practice of looking steadfastly to him, and all his excellencies, with a view to being changed, day by day, from one degree of glory to the next? Do you seek him in his word, and set your mind on him and his ways?

To all of this I invite you. Take up your Bible, the precious word of God. Call out to God in prayer for his illumination. Find, or freshly value, a Bible-believing church, and join those people in worship and study and service. Keep this focus until the Lord comes, or until he calls you home. Whatever afflictions may come, if Christ is more and more the bright and beautiful center of your life—if you walk in this light—they will never ruin the joyful orbits God has made for everything in your life—including money, sex, and power. Keep Christ as the blazing center, and you will be satisfied; the world will be served; and God will be glorified.

ACKNOWLEDGMENTS

This little book began with a big privilege. I was invited to speak to the Co-Mission weekend meetings called Revive in the summer of 2015 in Canterbury, England. The vision of Co-Mission is captured in the line "A Passion: For Planting, for London, for Christ." It is a church-planting movement in greater London. Speaking to their gathered churches was a great privilege, and meeting their leaders was very encouraging. I thank God for what I saw. The Coekin family showed Noël and me just the kind of hospitality we love.

My topic for that weekend was *Living in the Light: Money, Sex & Power*. Those messages have been expanded about threefold to become this book.

I am thankful to The Good Book Company for showing interest in the messages and providing insightful guidance for making them as useful as possible in book form.

David Mathis, Executive Editor at desiringGod.org, is indispensable in helping me move thoughts from head to paper to messages to books. This project would not have happened without him. Not for the first time.

The whole team at desiringGod.org, and the prayer team that supports me at our local church, are always helping with encouragement, support and intercession. God has been very kind to me. My prayer is that all of us would be protected from the pitfalls of money, sex, and power, and would bend their potentials for the glory of Christ and the good—especially the eternal good—of the church.

LIVE DIFFERENT

Many of us are serving, and feel like we're sinking. We feel joyless, weary and burdened. John Hindley shows how Jesus was telling the truth when he offered people an "easy yoke"—a way of serving him that is joyful and liberating. He explains why serving is so often joyless—and how our identity in Christ changes everything.

"This will transform the way you think about service. I wish I'd read it twenty years ago—buy it, read it, give it!"
Carrie Sandom, author of *Different by Design*

thegoodbook.com | thegoodbook.co.uk | thegoodbook.com.au

LIVEDIFFERENT

TIMOTHY LANE

LIVING
WITHOUT
WORRY

How to replace anxiety with peace

If you ever worry, you will want to read this book. Though anxiety is a familiar companion in our lives, it never becomes a welcome one. Timothy Lane offers real answers as he shows what worry is, why you feel it, and how you can replace it with an experience of real, lasting peace in all the ups and downs of your life.

"This book has helped me tremendously. May God help you conquer your worries as you read this book."
Clyde Christensen, Quarterback Coach, Indianapolis Colts

thegoodbook.com | thegoodbook.co.uk | thegoodbook.com.au

thegoodbook
COMPANY

thegoodbook
COMPANY
Opening up the Bible

At The Good Book Company, we are dedicated to helping Christians and local churches grow. We believe that God's growth process always starts with hearing clearly what he has said to us through his timeless word—the Bible.

Ever since we opened our doors in 1991, we have been striving to produce resources that honor God in the way the Bible is used. We have grown to become an international provider of user-friendly resources to the Christian community, with believers of all backgrounds and denominations using our Bible studies, books, evangelistic resources, DVD-based courses and training events.

We want to equip ordinary Christians to live for Christ day by day, and churches to grow in their knowledge of God, their love for one another, and the effectiveness of their outreach.

Call us for a discussion of your needs or visit one of our local websites for more information on the resources and services we provide.

Your friends at The Good Book Company

NORTH AMERICA   thegoodbook.com    866 244 2165
UK & EUROPE   thegoodbook.co.uk   0333 123 0880
AUSTRALIA   thegoodbook.com.au   (02) 6100 4211
NEW ZEALAND   thegoodbook.co.nz   (+64) 3 343 2463

 WWW.CHRISTIANITYEXPLORED.ORG
Our partner site is a great place for those exploring the Christian faith, with a clear explanation of the good news, powerful testimonies and answers to difficult questions.